# THE DIVINE INITIATIVE

# THE DIVINE INITIATIVE

David Ervin

**CCC Press**

**Belleville, Michigan**

*The Divine Initiative*



Published by CCC Press
44500 Willis Rd.,
Belleville, Michigan



First Printing, 2021

Italics or underlining in biblical quotes indicates emphasis added by the author.



ISBN 978-0-578-73100-1

Printed in the United States of America.

*To Jesus Christ*

*My Lord, my Savior, my everything;*
*Who took the initiative to seek and*
*to save this one who was lost.*

# Contents

# CHAPTER 1

# THE FIRST MOVE

My heart pounded as the evangelist called for a response. Against a mountain of fears and inhibitions, another force arose. A mysterious strength was welling up within me, taking captive my mind and will to the sweet call of the Savior. This unknown power, moving from my heart to my head to my body, transformed my thoughts and feelings into action. It was my very first act of obedience. I raised my trembling hand in response to the gospel.

I was a teenager attending a summer youth retreat. We camped outside for a whole week on the church grounds enjoying fun activities punctuated with group Bible studies. A life-changing event was certainly not on my agenda. My motive for attending the youth retreat was devoid of anything spiritual. I went because my friends were there, and more importantly, girls would be present. It was strictly a social occasion. The week's retreat culminated in a worship service. As a PK (that's a pastor's kid), I was all too familiar with the drill. It was time to "pay for the soup." They would bring in some itinerate evangelist who would preach at us for about forty-five minutes, and then we would be free to go.

Though reared in an evangelical Christian church, I was not a believer. I knew all the Bible stories and had heard the gospel message a thousand times, but it was a heap of foolishness to me. I thought Christianity was a crutch for the simple-minded to give them comfort. As an unbelieving PK, I had consequently become quite adept at getting through boring religious services and prepared myself for yet another routine mental blackout. But something was different this time. The setting was the same. The songs were the same. The message was the same. But something was vastly different.

I found myself hanging on every word. It seemed as if everything being said was just for me. I felt the weight of my sin and the need for the Savior like never before. The cross, unimportant to me the day before, suddenly became a refuge of safety. Prior to that hour, I considered Jesus Christ to be nothing more than a mildly curious religious figure. But at that moment, He leaped out of history and became personal as if He were alive and present in the room. I was acutely aware that He had done something real and stupendous on my behalf—something I did not deserve. When the evangelist called for us to raise a hand, indicating a response of faith in Christ, I raised mine.

I wish I could say that I steadfastly followed Jesus Christ from that day forward with unwavering faithfulness. That would make a great conversion story. But like many people, my coming to Jesus was like stepping across a blurred, gray line. Others may have experienced a sudden leap of faith; my journey was more like a gradual incline. Over the next few years, there would be many other incidents and "faith events." Somewhere along the way, I had crossed over to

Christ. Still, that day when I raised my hand represented a beginning—*a first move*. I had heard Christians say many times that "if you just take the first step, God will do the rest." Well, I had done my part. I took that first step. I had taken the initiative in this salvation thing.

But did I really make the first move? Was God waiting around for me to initiate His plan for my life, or was His plan already in motion? Was the raising of my hand the outward sign of my initiative in a relationship with God, or was it the culmination of a divine initiative that began in eternity past, moved a million circumstances, and overcame countless obstacles until at last it intersected with that specific moment in time?

The apostle John makes a causal statement about our love for God: "We love Him *because* He first loved us." (1 John 4:19). This is a profound truth yet one so simple that children sing about it in Sunday school: "O how I love Jesus, because He first loved me." According to John, there is a love prior to our love—a love that causes our love. There is a movement of God toward us that takes place long before our movement toward Him.

Perhaps as John wrote these things, the memory of Jesus' words rang in his mind. There in the upper room, Jesus said, "You did not choose Me, but I chose you" (John 15:16). On hearing this, the disciples might have protested, "But, Lord, we did choose you!" After all, they had left everything to follow Him. They had made a deliberate, free choice to abandon their former lives, their loved ones, their livelihood—everything to follow Jesus. They had indeed chosen Christ. So, what then did Jesus mean by this strange statement? The point is that as real and as important as their choice of Jesus was, it was nevertheless secondary. Christ's prior choice of them was ultimate. Yes, they made a real choice, but behind that choice was His.

Who was the ultimate cause of my hand lifting into the air in faith that day? On one level, of course, I was the cause. My mind understood, my heart gave assent, my will made a decision, and my body reacted. But it's not that simple. That day the room was full of other teens, each one hearing the same gospel message and presented with an identical opportunity to avail themselves of the benefits of Christ. I responded to the gospel, but most of them did not. By His grace, more than thirty years later I am still running hard after Jesus, but to my knowledge, most of the other teenagers present at that worship service are not.

Why me? Why did I respond in faith and they did not? Some try to answer this question by supposing that God grants everyone enough grace to make a decision for Christ possible. This is sometimes called "prevenient grace" because it is grace that comes *before* conversion. The idea is that God gives each person enough prevenient grace to overcome their sinful nature. [1] But does that solve the mystery? Prevenient grace gets us no closer to an answer. If the saved and unsaved man receives the same amount of prevenient grace, why does one cooperate with that grace while the other opposes it? What power enables the saved man to breach the barrier of his unbelief and lay hold of Christ?

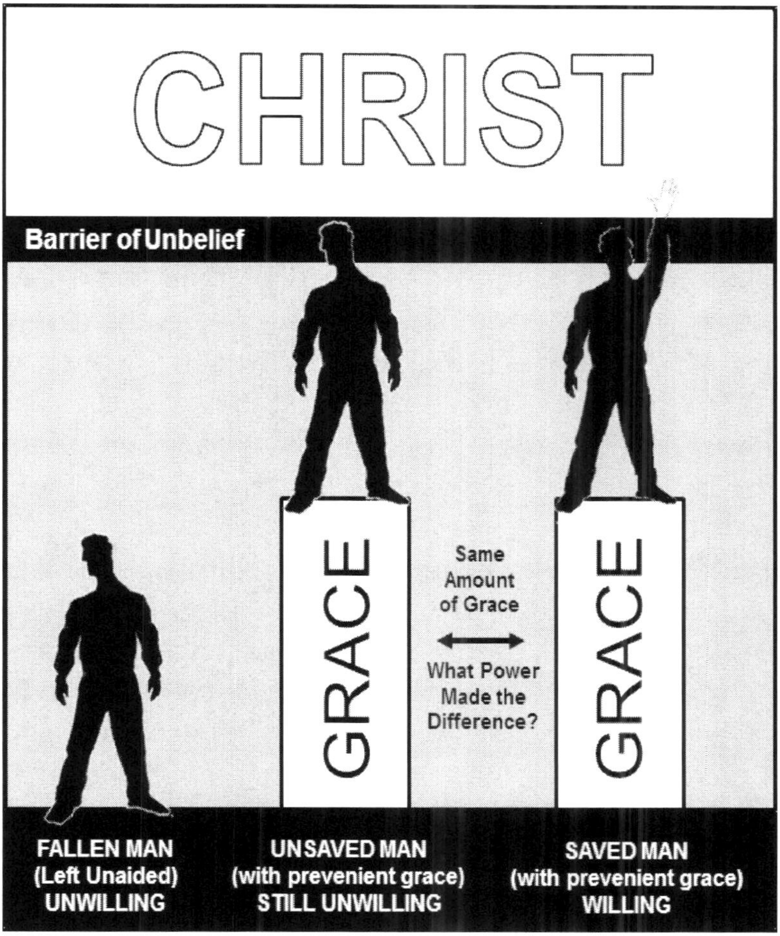

Equal doses of prevenient grace for all may seem like the simple solution, but it actually does nothing to help us understand why one person believes and another does not. The problem may be pushed back a little, but the underlying question remains—what makes the difference? Either the saved man received more grace than the other (in which case it would be the power of God that made the difference), or there is some quality in him that is lacking in the unsaved man (in which case it would be the power of man that made the difference).

Could any believer allow for the second possibility to be true? Was I wiser, more spiritual, more obedient, more intelligent, or more *whatever* than the other people in the room? That cannot be the case. If my response of faith is due to any quality found in me and not in them, I would have something to boast of. If I am the ultimate source of my faith, then salvation would not be owing to God's grace but rather to some property found in me that is not present in an unbeliever.[2] If this were true, my work of believing would be the critical factor in God's work of salvation. The power of salvation would then lie in me. The plans of God and the work of Christ would be impotent to save me without the prior addition of my work of faith. Regardless of what God accomplished on my behalf, I alone would possess the power to make His plans effectual. This is a far cry from the gospel that is "the power of God for salvation" (Romans 1:16 ESV).

Christian, on the last day, when you stand before God and look across the great chasm that will divide the sheep from the goats, what will you be able to point to that adequately explains why you are on the sheep side and someone else is on the goat side? You may say, "Because I believed in Christ, and they did not." Granted. But why did you believe in Christ and they did not? You reply, "Because I realized my lost condition." True. How is it that you came to that realization while they did not? What resources did you bring to bear that they somehow neglected? Do you not see that any quality, action, cooperation, response, or decision you cite as the *ultimate* explanation that separates you from them will redound to your merit? Yet on that great day of judgment, the difference between the sheep and the goats will be but grace alone. Grace demands, therefore, that the reason we believed and they did not is because of something outside of us, something antecedent to our choice, something that has no basis in what we have done or will ever do.

A crowd once asked Jesus, "'What shall we do, that we may work *the works* of God?' Jesus answered and said to them, 'This is the work of God, that you *believe* in Him who He sent'" (John 6:28–29). This conversation was about work—spiritual work. The crowd wanted to know the spiritual labor God requires for us to be in right standing with Him. Perhaps they were looking for a seven-step process or a list of religious deeds that must be accomplished to get to heaven. Instead, Jesus told them that the spiritual work God requires is to believe in Him! Faith in Christ is the great work that lays hold of salvation and transports us out of darkness and into the kingdom of God.

So then, according to Jesus, the seemingly simple act of my lifting a hand in faith represented a spiritual work. In fact, it was the greatest spiritual work of my life. It was a work that connected me to all the benefits of Christ's atonement and determined where I will spend eternity. In that moment of belief, a spiritual labor was accomplished that determined my forever. Who did that work? Who was it that achieved in my heart what Jesus called "the works of God"? There are only three options:

1. It was all my work
2. It was a mixture of God's work and my work
3. It was all God's work

The first option gives me all the credit for my salvation. In option number two, the credit is divided between the Divinity and me. The third option gives all the credit to God. No Christian would attribute the work of their salvation to themselves or even dare share the glory with God. We know in our hearts that He did it all. It is all God's work because repentance and saving faith does not ultimately originate in the believer; they are gifts of God.

We have no platform from which to boast in our salvation because even the very faith we exercise to connect with Christ is given to us freely by His grace.

| **Repentance and Faith Are Gifts of God** |
|---|
| "For to you it has been *granted* on behalf of Christ, not only *to believe* in Him, but also to suffer for His sake" **Philippians 1:29** |
| "in humility correcting those who are in opposition, if God perhaps will *grant* them *repentance*" **2 Timothy 2:25** |
| "God has also *granted* to the Gentiles *repentance* to life." **Acts 11:18** |

The apostle Paul explains in Ephesians 2:8 that "by grace you have been saved through faith." Faith is the instrument that connects us to the saving work of Christ. Faith makes us a beneficiary of the cross. Paul then goes on to clarify that this faith is "not of yourselves; it is the gift of God." Paul is careful to explain that even the initial work of believing is not a labor produced from resources within ourselves but is something given to us. He understood that if faith originates in us, we would have grounds to boast and salvation would not be of grace. That is why, after explaining that faith is a gift, he goes on to say in verse 9, "Not of works, lest anyone should boast."

Because God is the *author* of our faith (Hebrews 12:2), the last scrap of human merit is removed, and God receives all the glory. Our faith is His work in us.

Faith as the gift of God also explains why some believe and others do not. Quite simply, God does not give this gift to everyone. If God gave the gift of faith and repentance to everyone, then everyone would repent and believe. It was self-evident to the apostle Paul that since the Christians in Philippi believed, they must then have been granted the ability to believe (Philippians 1:29). According to Jesus, the reason for the Pharisees' unbelief was that they had not been granted faith: "Therefore *they could not believe*, because Isaiah said again: 'He has blinded their eyes and hardened their hearts, lest they should see with their eyes, lest they should understand with their hearts and turn, so that I should heal them.'" (John 12:39–40).

A gift is, by definition, something freely given. Suppose I went to the shopping mall and decided to give five people a twenty-dollar bill just because I'm feeling gracious. Could the other people in the mall then justly say, "That's not right! Where's our twenty bucks? You gave it to them, so you have to give it to us too!" Of course, that is ridiculous. I didn't owe them a gift in the first place. That's the same argument my first-grade teacher used when I gave a piece of gum to my best buddy. "If you don't have enough for the whole class, then put it away," she said. But with all due respect to Mrs. Heatherly, just because I give a gift to one (or some) does not mean I now owe a gift to all. A gift is never owed.

God made us and gave us every good thing we enjoy. We are showered with His goodness and breathe in His blessings every single day. And yet the universal response of the human race is to reject God and suppress our knowledge of Him (Romans 1:19–21). What principle obligates God to stop His enemies from despising Him? There is none. The sovereign God has every right (and would be entirely just) to leave us in our rebellion if He chooses to do so. It is the wonder of His mercy that He intervenes to turn some of His enemies into friends.

When I responded to the call of the evangelist that day, it was because of an appointment. Another evangelist, Luke, explains when he describes what happened to a similar crowd: "When the Gentiles heard this [the gospel], they were glad and glorified the word of the Lord. And *as many as had been appointed to eternal life believed*" (Acts 13:48). God had made a prior appointment for some of the people in that crowd to believe. When we consider the depth of our sin and how grievously we have offended God, we should not be amazed that God gives the gift of faith only to some. What should astound us is that He gives this grace to anyone at all.

Long before you and I made our first move toward Christ, God had from all eternity made the first move toward us:

> Just as He chose us in Him before the foundation of the world, that we should be holy and without blame before Him in love, having predestined us to adoption as sons by Jesus Christ to Himself, according to the good pleasure of His will (Ephesians 1:4–5).

| **Ephesians 1:4–5** | |
|---|---|
| God has chosen a people for Himself. | **"He chose us in Him"** |
| The purpose of that choice is salvation in Christ. | **"to adoption as sons by Jesus Christ to Himself"** |
| God made that choice before we were born and could deserve it. | **"He chose us in Him before the foundation of the world."** |

Ages before I made my choice of Christ, God had made a choice of me. The same is true of every one of the redeemed. Someone may object, "But doesn't God choose everybody?" To choose everything is to make no choice at all. To choose is, by definition, to limit one's selection within a particular category. It is to select something (or someone) while passing over another.

According to Scripture, there is no question that God chooses some for salvation. "God from the beginning *chose you* for salvation" (2 Thessalonians 2:13).

The word "elect" is found seventeen times in the New Testament as a description of those God chose for salvation and seven times as a verb meaning to choose someone for salvation. There are other words and references to this concept as well.

| Examples of Election in Scripture |
| --- |
| "Unless the Lord had shortened those days, no flesh would be saved; but for the **elect's** sake, whom He **chose**, He shortened the days." (Mark 13:20) |
| "Who shall bring a charge against God's **elect**?" (Romans 8:33) |
| "knowing, beloved brethren, your **election** by God" (1 Thessalonians 1:4) |
| "To the . . . **elect** according to the foreknowledge of God the Father" (1 Peter 1:1–2) |
| "These will make war with the Lamb, and the Lamb will overcome them, for He is Lord of lords and King of kings; and those who are with Him are called, **chosen**, and faithful." (Revelation 17:14) |

References to God's choice of an elect people for salvation abound in Scripture. So then the question is not "Does God choose people for salvation?" but "On *what basis* does God choose people for salvation?"

Some would say that God looks ahead in time and sees us choosing Him, and then on the basis of our decision, He chooses us.[3] That only brings us back to the original problem: Why did I choose Christ and they didn't? What attribute exists in the believer (but is absent in the unbeliever) that causes them to choose God in the first place? If God looks ahead in time to see *anything* in you that provokes His salvific response, it is to that quality you owe your eternal salvation. Playing a shell game with God's knowledge of the future does nothing to change the underlying fact: in this way of thinking, you achieved something that the unbeliever did not, and it is on the basis of what you did that God chose you for salvation.

On the contrary, according to apostle Paul, God's choice has nothing to do with any quality found in us, but it was "according to the good pleasure of His will" (Ephesians 1:5). God does nothing arbitrarily. He has a perfect and holy reason for His choices, hidden within His sovereign purposes. As is His divine prerogative, God has not presently revealed the full reasons behind His choices. But He has told us what the reason is *not*. It has nothing to do with anything found in us. "[God] has saved us and called us with a holy calling, *not according to our works, but according to His own purpose and grace* which was given to us in Christ Jesus before time began" (2 Timothy 1:9).

We deserved no part in this. We caused no part in this. We accomplished no part in this—God did it all, and He did it for His glory. Charles Spurgeon, that great prince of preachers, testifies of this truth when he recalls his conversion:

> One week-night, when I was sitting in the house of God, I was not thinking much about the preacher's sermon, for I did not believe it. The thought struck me, "*How did you come to be a Christian?*" I sought the Lord. "*But how did you come to seek the Lord?*" The truth flashed across my mind in a moment—I should not have sought Him unless there had been some previous influence in my mind to *make me* seek Him. I prayed, thought I, but then I asked myself, "*How came I to pray?*" I was induced to pray by reading the Scriptures. "*How came I to read the Scriptures?*" I did read them, but what led me to do so? Then, in a moment, I saw that God was at the bottom of it all and that He was the Author of my faith, and so the whole doctrine of grace opened up to me, and from that doctrine, I have not departed to this day, and I desire to make this my constant confession, "I ascribe my change wholly to God."[4]

There are thousands of events that God uses along the way in a believer's journey. There are some things that God has done and some things that we have done. Sometimes it's hard to sort it all out. May I suggest it is as simple as this, "I once was lost, and now I am found." In the final analysis, the one responsible for that transition is not you. I think every saved person knows that deep inside. If you are a Christian, why do you thank God for your conversion? Because you know deep down in your bones that He did it. It is not that I chose God, and in response to that work, He chose me. God chose me first, and His divine initiative is what enabled me to choose Him that day at the youth retreat—and every day after that. God made the first move.

# CHAPTER 2

# SPIRITUALLY DEAD

Jesus stood before the grave of Lazarus. The Scripture reports that He was "deeply moved" (John 11:33 ESV), also translated, "He groaned in the spirit." It was as if there were a visceral rage inside Jesus toward death itself that shook Him to the core, and He who is the resurrection and the life had come to do something about it. This Death Destroyer stood before the tomb like a champion in the arena stands before his foe. A sharp command was issued: "Lazarus, come forth!" (v. 43). But the corpse of Lazarus could not obey that command. It could not hear the words of Jesus. It could not make a decision to obey Him. It could not animate itself to meet the demands of this divine imperative now ringing through the tomb. Lazarus had no ability to cooperate with Jesus. He could not "just take that first step, and God will do the rest." He could not because he was dead—four days dead. The resurrection power of Christ had to first make Lazarus alive before he could will and act on the command of Jesus.

As it goes with Lazarus, so it goes with us. In the Scriptures, one of the key metaphors God uses to describe our condition as we come into this world is that we are "dead in trespasses and sins" (Ephesians 2:1; Colossians 2:13). It is telling that God chose the image of a dead man to picture our condition outside of Christ. God could have described us as merely sick or even dying. As bad as that diagnosis might be, there remains the possibility that we could aid and contribute to our recovery. To be sure, if we are sick we need a doctor to save us. But even in such a state we are not helpless. We can still cooperate with the doctor. There lies within us the ability to take the prescribed medicine.[5] But what aid can we give in the morgue? What cooperation can a dead man give? In our flesh, we flatter ourselves to think we can make a contribution. Oh, it's okay if we get a bit of help from above—a little spiritual boost perhaps—so long as we can do our part. Yet God holds the spiritual mirror of His Word before us and bids us to look at a reality we desperately do not want to see. The diagnosis of our condition is far worse than we thought. We're dead. We have no spiritual ability to make any move whatsoever toward God. The gospel command goes out, "Come to Christ!" But like Lazarus, we have no ability to obey that command unless God first takes the initiative to resurrect us.

But why is this our condition? We certainly didn't start that way. When God made the first man, He breathed life into him, and he became a living soul. Adam was alive physically and spiritually. He had the capacity to want and delight in his Creator.

God placed Adam under a test. Though every good thing was freely given to our first dad, there was one prohibition. True, it was a ban on a certain kind of produce, but it could have been pretty much anything. It could have been "Don't cross that river" or "Don't stay out past eleven o'clock." Any barrier would do.

This was not about fruit—this was about sovereignty. This test was about who would be God.

The temptation offered to Adam, vicariously through his wife as he sheepishly listened in on her conversation with Satan, was that he would be like God (Genesis 3:4). But more than any other creature, he was already like God. Adam was made as an image-bearer of his Creator. It was his duty and privilege to reflect the character of God to the world. But it was not enough for Adam to be like God. He wanted to *be* God. The penalty for violation was death, and if that seems over the top, consider what was really going on in his heart. This was a grasping at autonomy—to throw off the shackles of God's rule and ownership. Adam's rebellion was an attempted heavenly *coup d'état* in hopes of dethroning the King of the universe. A collision was taking place between the will of man and the will of God. Somebody was going to die.[6]

It was the most selfish, and despicable decision that could ever be made—to rebel against the One who gave him everything. Yet Adam did rebel. In so doing, he stopped believing God is good and that it is good to be under His authority.

Instead of finding freedom, Adam became a prisoner. A radical change took place in his very nature. In that dark descent, two things happened for the first time: Adam realized he was naked, and he ran from his Maker. Hidden in the shadows, Adam sensed something had shattered his relationship with God. Fellowship was lost. The breach seemed beyond repair.

Perhaps you may be thinking, "A sad story, no doubt, but so what? Why should I care about the tragic fall of this man that took place so long ago?" The Scripture responds that Adam's sin was your sin and the consequences of his crime have fallen on you.

In this drama of Eden, God was placing the entire human race on trial. Adam not only acted for himself but stood as a representative of all his descendants. "Just as through one man sin entered the world, and death through sin, and thus death spread to all men" (Romans 5:12). Think of it as a class-action lawsuit. Say, for example, some company's product allegedly harms fifty thousand people. The courts do not then hold fifty thousand trials. Instead, the court tries one representative case. Whatever the outcome of this single trial will be the outcome of all. So too, in Adam, God put humanity on trial, and the court of heaven declared that Adam's verdict would be yours. The result of this one offense was that "judgment came to all men, resulting in condemnation" (Romans 5:18).

It is just for God to hold you personally culpable because Adam represented you. Guilt by representation is not as strange as it may seem. If a person hires a hit man to murder someone, for example, that person can be convicted of first-degree murder, even though they didn't personally pull the trigger. This is a just judgment because the hit man represented their intentions. The protest arises, "But I didn't pick Adam to represent me!" And the secret boast is "If I had been there, things would have been different." But do not forget that the One who picked Adam to represent you is God. God's choices are morally perfect and made with infallible knowledge. God chose the first man. He arranged this trial in such a way that Adam did the same thing you and I would have done if we had been there. Any denial of this truth can be quickly quashed by looking at our record. As soon as we were old enough to do so, each one of us personally violated God's commands. In so doing, we demonstrated our solidarity with Adam and proved that his actions stood in perfect unity with our intentions. Adam so completely represented you that in the mind of God, *you were there*. It was you who took the fruit. It was you who flagrantly stepped over the boundaries of your Sovereign. And it was you who justly reaped the consequences of that choice.[7]

What then are the consequences? God had clearly warned that death would follow a breach of contract. This certainly includes physical death, but it goes far deeper. From that day forward, the children of Adam would be born *spiritually* dead. It is not a pretty picture, but let us look into God's Word and view the wreckage of the fall.

## Dead from the Womb

> "Even from birth the wicked go astray; from the womb they are wayward." (Psalm 58:3)

> "I was sinful at birth, sinful from the time my mother conceived me." (Psalm 51:5 NIV)

No one has to teach a child to lie or be selfish. The qualities of sin emerge from within as quickly as our young bodies and minds can accommodate them. God originally made us with a nature that leans in His direction. The consequence of the fall is to be born with a disposition that runs away from God. When we look at a newborn baby, it is hard to imagine that this is a rebel at war with God. From our perspective, we only see innocence. But though a child is *relatively* innocent when compared with an adult, from the perspective of God, he or she has simply not had enough opportunity to act on their sinful inclinations. Given enough time, their true colors will show. Every new mother should be forewarned in the maternity ward, "One day, your baby will insult you." Contrary to the idea that we come into this world morally neutral, the Scripture paints a picture of a heart that is, from the womb, biased toward sin. Left in this condition, the fallen man will continue to run from God all his life.

## Dead Mind

> But the natural man does not receive the things of the Spirit of God, for they are foolishness to him; nor can he know them, because they are spiritually discerned. (1 Corinthians 2:14)

> Because the carnal mind is enmity against God; for it is not subject to the law of God, nor indeed can be. (Romans 8:7)

The human mind is fearfully and wonderfully made. It is capable of astonishing heights of complex thought. Yet it too is spiritually dead on arrival. Though the fallen mind can create smartphones, and send men to the moon, it cannot grasp the simple truth of the gospel. In its damaged condition, the truth of Jesus will sound like foolishness. The fallen mind, if left in this state, will never understand or *receive the things of the Spirit of God.* What is the source of this lack of understanding? The fallen mind is at *enmity* [hostile] *against God.* This is not a case of honest misunderstanding. This is a willful refusal to hear the truth, born out of a heart filled with hostility toward the Truth-Bearer. Notice the passages above speak of what the fallen mind cannot do. There lies within our fallen flesh a built-in animosity toward God that makes it utterly impossible to submit to His will. "Why do you not understand My speech?" asked Jesus. "Because you are *not able* to listen to My word" (John 8:43).

## Dead Will

> There is none who understands; There is none who seeks after God. (Romans 3:11)

In recent years, a movement within evangelicalism has arisen with a very noble goal: to attract more people to church so that they might hear and respond to the gospel. To achieve this desired outcome, some have turned to the methods of modern marketing. Perhaps the same finely tuned techniques used to sell cars could be just as effective "selling" the gospel. The idea is that masses of people are out there in the world seeking God but they just don't know where to find Him, and what the church needs to do is figure out what these *seekers* want and then market Christ to meet their felt needs. By studying demographics and taking surveys, the church can determine what the population's perceived needs are. It can then tweak and reform itself to appeal to those needs. The seeker will then beat a path to the church door where they will find *seeker-sensitive* services. The music is loud and hip, served up with gourmet coffee and a short sermon trimmed of any mention of sin, wrath, or other seeker-offending concepts. They are dazzled by the presentation and turn to Christ. All this is a fine idea born out of sincere motives, but there is just one little problem: according to Scripture, no one seeks God.

One of the tragic consequences of the fall is the corruption of the will itself. Iniquity has seeped into our very ability to make spiritual choices. It is naive to think that the sin nature infects our bodies and minds but the will somehow emerged from the train wreck of the fall unscathed and untouched. The will is not a neutral and unbiased organism that operates independently of the nature of man. The will follows the heart. And a fallen heart will always produce fallen choices. After Eden, we lost the ability to *want rightly*. Sin contaminates all our decisions.

Any Christian who is even vaguely familiar with the biblical doctrine of the fall will readily acknowledge that the will is damaged. But even a damaged will can still function, right? Though it may be sputtering along on three cylinders, there remains enough power to churn out at least one spiritually good decision. A damaged will may still have sufficient capacity to incline itself to Christ. But the pages of Scripture write the obituary to the fallen will. It is not merely damaged; it, too, is dead. It is unable to choose Christ unless God first takes the initiative.

Jesus speaks of this reality when He says, "No one can come to Me unless it has been granted to him by My Father" (John 6:65). Again the Scripture speaks of what man cannot do as a result of the consequences of the fall. This is not about permission. The gospel invitation goes out to all. The Savior calls to the world, "If anyone thirsts, let him come to Me and drink" (John 7:37). What is in view here is not what a person may do but what they can do. According to

Jesus, no fallen person has the ability to come to Christ (i.e., come to Christ in faith for salvation), unless God first intervenes and *grants* them the capacity to do so. Jesus makes it clear that except a prior operation of God takes place to change and empower the fallen will, no one is able to believe on Him.

What is it exactly that makes the fallen will unable to come to Christ? What is this defect that moves Jesus to describe the will as impotent to incline itself to the Savior? It is the nature of the will itself. The will is our ability to select the most desired alternative of the moment. In the face of millions of choices every day, the will weighs the available options and then chooses what is most desirable given the situation at hand. To put it simply, the will chooses what it wants. The will must always choose what it wants. It can do no other since that is its job. Someone may object, "Ah, but I don't want to get up on Monday morning and go to work—I would choose to sleep in if I had my will in the matter!" All things being equal, you would choose to stay in bed. But given a choice between eating every day or going hungry, you want to work. The will always selects the most desirable option available at the time.

Consider the reason why you are reading this book right now. Among the many different activities available, you decided that reading this sentence is the most favorable option of the moment. A multitude of conscious and subconscious reasons moved you to this decision. In other words, you are reading this because you want to. But I suppose you could be reading this book because some crazed preacher dude kidnapped you, locked you in a prison cell, and said, "I'm not letting you out until you read this." Have you heard of prison ministry? This is taking it to the next level! In that situation, you might say, "I am reading this book against my will." But even in such an extreme scenario, you are still choosing what you want. You are still opting for the most favorable outcome, given the available choices. When faced with further incarceration or reading this book, you chose the latter because the will must always elect what is most desirable at the time. The will must always choose what it wants. So then what does the fallen man want? In a word—sin.

When God looks at the fallen man, He observes that every inclination of the thoughts of his heart is only evil all the time (Genesis 6:5). Jesus' assessment is no more flattering. He says to fallen men, "You are of your father the devil, and the desires of your father you want to do" (John 8:44). The consequence of the fall is to be born with a disposition that will not step into the light because the fallen will "[loves] darkness rather than light" (John 3:19). It is to possess a dead heart that is "deceitful above all things and desperately wicked" (Jeremiah 17:9).

So then, if the will always chooses what it wants, and the fallen will always wants sin, then the fallen man is morally unable to want Christ. We do not seek what we do not desire. The essence of salvation is to want Christ. It is to desire Him, delight in Him, find in Him all that is lovely and satisfying. But you cannot cause yourself to want what you do not want. "We cannot find God for the same reason a thief can't find a police officer."[8]

But someone objects, "The Bible teaches that we have a free will!" Indeed it does: "Choose for yourselves this day whom you will serve" (Joshua 24:15); "Whoever desires, let him take the water of life freely" (Revelation 22:17). Passages like these are legion. Our will is free (meaning that the will is free to choose what it wants), and it is that very freedom that enslaves the fallen person. Because the will that is fallen only desires the anti-God and always chooses the anti-God. Left to its own devices, the fallen will freely and without coercion will choose the sin that holds it captive every single time. The Bible describes our condition in Adam as "slaves of sin" (Romans 6:17) and in "the snare of the devil" (2 Timothy 2:26) precisely because, apart from God changing our desires, we are unable to want anything other than the sin that ensnares and holds us as a prisoner. Left to our fallen inclinations, we cannot come to Christ because we do not want Christ. The fallen will is powerless to desire the Savior. If anyone is to look to Christ, God must first give that person *the want* for Christ.

I once had a conversation with an unbelieving man in which I tried to help him understand his fallen condition. He objected to the idea that he was spiritually dead and, apart from God's gracious intervention, unable to choose Christ. "I can come to Christ anytime I want to!" he argued.

"Then do it now," I challenged him.

"I don't want to."

"Exactly."

When most people think of free will, they imagine a will that is neutral and independent. To be truly free, they reason, the will must be able to turn in either direction without any outside force determining which way it will go. However, "true freedom is not the liberty to do anything we please, but the liberty to do what we ought,"[9] and that is something the fallen will cannot do. Though the will may be free to choose, it is not free from its own nature. The will can only choose what is in agreement with its nature. Put a bowl of oatmeal and a big raw steak in front of a hungry lion, and he will choose the meat every time. That is not because the lion is incapable of eating oatmeal. If oatmeal were the only thing to eat, eventually, the lion would eat it. But give him a choice between oats and flesh, and he must always make the same choice—according to his nature.[10]

The same is true of all freewill agents, whether it be lions, angels, humans, or even God! Even God must choose according to His own perfect nature. When the Bible says that God "cannot lie" (Titus 1:2) or that He "cannot deny Himself" (2 Timothy 2:13), it is not suggesting some deficiency in God's ability. When the Scripture speaks of what God cannot do, it is revealing something about the will of God—it always acts in accordance with His righteous character. Therefore, it is impossible for God to choose what is contrary to His own nature.

That is a glorious truth about God, but it is a dire predicament for the fallen sons of Adam. Except for God's intervention, we too can only choose what is in accordance with our sin nature. Bad trees, said Jesus, cannot produce good fruit (Matthew 7:17). "Can the Ethiopian change his skin or the leopard its spots?" (Jeremiah 13:23). The fallen man is not able to choose Christ because Christ is contrary to his fundamental delight. He has no more power to change his nature than a leopard can exchange its spots for zebra stripes.

We are born dead as a judgment for our rebellion in the garden, with a dead mind that cannot understand Christ and a dead will that cannot want Christ. When this spiritual cadaver is presented with the gospel command to repent and believe, it cannot obey, just as the corpse of Lazarus could not obey the command of Jesus to exit the tomb.

But here's the way it works in resurrections, both physical and spiritual: *God grants what He commands.*

God commands us to do what we cannot do—come to Christ and live. Then He graciously gives us the ability to obey. Along with the command to exit the tomb came a prior resurrection power that caused the dead heart of Lazarus to begin to beat. Blood began to course through his veins. Neurons began to fire. Decayed cells sprang to life, and Lazarus got up and walked out. And it is a good thing that Jesus called Lazarus by name, or all the dead would have stood up! Lazarus is but a picture of the divine initiative that moves upon all who pass from death to life. What happened physically to Lazarus happens spiritually to all the Redeemed. A resurrection happens every time dead men and women rise—repent—and believe. “The hour is coming, and now is, when the dead will hear the voice of the Son of God, and those who hear will live” (John 5:25).

# CHAPTER 3

# THE NEW MAN

"Do not marvel that I said to you, 'You must be born again'" (John 3:7). So said Jesus to Nicodemus. And given what we have seen about the fallen condition, we should not be surprised either. It follows that since we come into this world dead on arrival, we are well beyond resuscitation. The fallen mind cannot understand the gospel. The fallen will cannot want the gospel. If anyone is to be saved, God must first make a change in our very nature. Dead men do not need reformation—nothing short of regeneration will do.

Regeneration is the act of God by which He supernaturally causes the human heart to seek out what it did not want before. It is when God gives you the *want*. In regeneration, God fills the sinner with desires that were not previously there: a desire to love, honor, and worship God and for the hallowing of His name.[11] This is not about making religious resolutions; regeneration is a miracle inside whereby God the Holy Spirit causes His former enemies to turn from sin, run to the Savior, and live for the praise of His glory.

God does not choose His metaphors willy-nilly. We would do well to pay close attention to the labels the Holy Spirit attaches to spiritual realities. The Bible uses several images to describe regeneration. Let's consider four of them: new birth, new heart, new creation, and new life.

## New Birth

In his 1976 campaign for the presidency, Jimmy Carter described himself publicly as a "born-again Christian."[12] The media was abuzz as this strange new term entered the popular American vocabulary. For many people, a born-again Christian means someone who identifies with the evangelical brand of Christianity. That's the charitable definition. For others, born-again is synonymous with a religious fanatic. For them, there are the normal Christians, and then there are those crazy, born-again Christians.

But in His nighttime conversation with Nicodemus, Jesus reveals there is, in fact, only one kind of Christian: "Most assuredly, I say to you, unless one is born again, he cannot see the kingdom of God" (John 3:3). The apostles also make frequent use of this idea of the new birth (1 Peter 1:23; 1 John 3:9), describing the Christian as one who has been born a second time, or "born of God" (1 John 5:18). We may flatter ourselves with the idea that though we are certainly not perfect, there must be something salvageable in us. Surely there is at least a trace of goodness within that can be redeemed. This delusion is shattered into a thousand pieces when we hear the divine prequalification to salvation: "You must be born again." To enter the kingdom of God requires nothing less than a total do-over.

## New Heart

When God gave the law to Israel, He promised to bless the nation on the condition of obedience. But no provision was given to change the people's hearts. It was an external call to obey without any promise of an inward conversion. That is no fault on the part of the law—it just isn't in the law's job description. The relationship between unregenerate people and the law always works like this: "Law comes to him from the outside and imposes standards on him that he hates. Law tells him what he ought to do but gives him neither the desire nor the power to do it."[13] Is it any wonder that stony hearts failed to obey God?

Compare this to the promise of the New Covenant. In addition to the command to obey, God promises to supply a new heart, filled with desire for Him: "I will give you a new heart and put a new spirit within you; I will take the heart of stone out of your flesh and give you a heart of flesh. I will put My Spirit within you and cause you to walk in My statutes" (Ezekiel 36:26–27). Stone hearts will never beat for God. Stone hearts will never pump with love for the law because they despise the Lawmaker. If anyone is to turn to the Savior, there must first be a divine heart transplant. Suddenly, the sinner who could see no beauty in Christ before now runs to Him, as did Lydia, the seller of purple. "The Lord *opened her heart to heed* the things spoken by Paul" (Acts 16:14).

## New Creation

Just in case we start thinking that regeneration is merely a new arrangement of something already inside us, the Scripture also uses the imagery of a new creation. “If anyone is in Christ, he is a new creation” (2 Corinthians 5:17). The apostle Paul in 2 Corinthians 4:6 brings to mind the primordial command of Genesis and compares it to the work of regeneration: “For it is the God who commanded light to shine out of darkness, who has shone in our hearts to give the light of the knowledge of the glory of God in the face of Jesus Christ.”

When we humans create, we are not really making anything new. Our creations are just rearrangements of the stuff that is already there. The artist may paint, and the sculptor may sculpt, but God replies, “Try that from scratch!” God is the only being who creates *ex nihilo* (out of nothing). When the Bible calls the believer a “new creation,” it means just that—out of nothing. Just as God brings forth the first creation from nothing, He makes the new creation from that same nothing. The Maker of the universe need not look for raw materials in us to bring saving faith into existence. God speaks into the darkness of the fallen soul and, by the sheer force of His word, brings into being that which was not previously there. Repentance, faith, desire for Christ—all these qualities leap from the void the moment the Creator says, “Let there be…”

## New Life

In chapter 2, we came face-to-face with the Bible's description of fallen human beings: "[You] were dead in trespasses and sins" (Ephesians 2:1). If that were God's final word about us, we would be utterly without hope. But mercy intervened to supply what we needed most—resurrection! "But God, who is rich in mercy, because of His great love with which He loved us, even when we were dead in trespasses *made us alive* together with Christ" (Ephesians 2:4–5). If spiritual death is our primary malady, then regeneration is the provision of grace by which dead men and women come to life again. "And you, being dead in your trespasses and the uncircumcision of your flesh, He has made alive together with Him" (Colossians 2:13). Dead minds and dead wills now divinely quickened run to embrace the Savior.

## The Common Thread

New birth, new heart, new creation, new life—each one of these biblical images of regeneration helps us to understand this great work of God from a slightly different angle. But do they have anything in common? Are there any shared qualities? By putting this multifaceted imagery together, a complete picture emerges. Let's look at the common thread the Scripture weaves into the fabric of regeneration.

## Regeneration Is Passive

How much did you contribute to your first birth? If your coming into this world was anything like mine, I'd say your role in the whole affair was exactly nothing. Our contribution to our second birth amounts to the same—zero. Consider again the metaphors God has chosen to describe regeneration (new birth, new creation, new heart, resurrection). What do these images have in common? The subjects are all passive. Babies do not assist their mothers as they give them birth. Creatures do not aid the Creator in His work of creation. A cadaver has no ability to resurrect itself. And human beings cannot cause their hearts to want what it does not desire. Do you think God is trying to tell us something here? Each of these biblical images points to the utterly passive nature of man in the work of regeneration. This inward transformation is something done to the sinner, outside of the sinner, and apart from his or her help or cooperation.

This passivity follows from what we have seen of the nature of fallen flesh. Since we are spiritually dead, then, of course, God is the only active player in regeneration. If God looked ahead in time to see what the dead sinner would do on his own, He would observe him doing precisely nothing. That is what corpses do. The dead do not work, contribute, or cooperate.

The apostle John tells us that we are born into the kingdom "not of blood, nor of the will of the flesh, nor of the will of man, but of God" (John 1:13). Clearly, this kind of birth does not come about by human decision [14] God's will is the decisive force in regeneration, which destroys any remnant of humblebrag I have left. "Yes, I was lost, but thank God I had enough sense to look and live!" The gospel puts to death that boast when it tells me that my desire for Christ is owed entirely to His quickening! The dead are made alive not because of any participation on their part but because God has raised them in Christ (Colossians 3:1). Our passivity in regeneration sings the praises of God and redounds to His glory.

## Regeneration Precedes Faith

The various illustrations used in Scripture to describe regeneration all point to an initiating event that precedes any action on the part of the Christian. The baby is born before she can cry out to her mother. The dead man is resurrected before he can take one step toward Christ. In the same way, God regenerates the sinner prior to the sinner turning to Christ in faith.

A common misunderstanding in the evangelical church today is that a sinner must first come to Christ in faith and repentance before he or she can be born again. In this way of thinking, being born again is a transformation that takes place immediately after (or almost instantly upon) conversion. Jesus' imperative, "You must be born again," is heard by many to mean "You must come to Christ, and then you will be born again"—or in some southern circles, "You gotta get born'd again." So then, the typical view is that one first believes and then regeneration comes after. In his book *How to Be Born Again* Billy Graham states, "Thus, repentance is first, and absolutely necessary if we are to be born again."[15] I do realize that in popular evangelicalism it is tantamount to committing the unforgivable sin to contradict the late Mr. Graham. But with all due respect to his legacy, how can a heart of stone repent and believe on Christ unless it is first changed into a heart of flesh? As we have seen, regeneration (or being born again) is the very act by which God changes the heart so that it grieves of sin and desires the Savior. How, then, can a sinner repent before they are given a repentant heart? If ever there were an effort to put the cart in front of the horse, it is the idea that the sinner can choose Christ before God gives him the desire in the new birth to do so. The very title of Mr. Graham's book begs the question of how I can do *anything* to initiate my own birth.

One must first be born again, and only then will one turn from sin and believe on Christ. But the idea that a person can *act* spiritually before he *exists* spiritually, that he can behave before he is born, is to embrace the impossible.[16] Thus, one can no more tell someone how to be born again than to instruct a preborn infant on how to come into the world. For a person to savingly believe on Christ is to demonstrate that regeneration has already taken place. Faith is the evidence of an awakened heart. The Scripture puts it like this: "Whoever believes that Jesus is the Christ *is* born of God" (1 John 5:1). That little word "is" represents a present state of being. Those who believe on Christ do so because they are already born of God. According to John, saving faith is not the cause of regeneration, but it is the outward evidence that regeneration has already taken place. Saving faith does not produce the new birth—just the opposite—the new birth produces saving faith.

Before I am accused of splitting the proverbial theological hair, please understand there is a spiritual danger inherent in this misunderstanding. This belief that faith precedes the new birth (sometimes called decisional regeneration) can lead to a subtle form of works salvation. It undermines the biblical teaching that the sinner is utterly helpless regarding the matter of salvation to do anything to remedy his situation. Rather than being powerless and at the mercy of God, decisional regeneration places all the power in the sinner's own will. God stands ready to do His part, to be sure, but is impotent to act until the rebel provides the key component—his choice. In decisional regeneration, the difference between life and death is owed finally to the sinner's action, not God's saving mercy. It follows, then, that this view also weakens the true depth of human depravity, suggesting that the fallen man is not totally lost but, rather, within his breast resides just enough insight for him to find his way to Christ. But if we rightly understand regeneration to precede faith, it becomes clear that this cannot be. The unregenerate man will never come to Christ prior to regeneration because he does not *want* Christ prior to regeneration (John 6:65). The prison door is open wide, but the fallen man chooses to remain in the captivity of his sin.

How can God command a man to come to Christ when he is morally impotent to do so? Because "with men this is impossible, but with God all things are possible" (Matthew 19:26). The gospel is never about what man can do. The good news is about what God can do. God accompanies His command with the supernatural ability to obey it. God does this by replacing our stony, unbelieving heart with a fleshy heart that runs hard after Jesus. God commands the worm to fly, and then in the miracle of new birth, a metamorphosis takes place—God transforms the caterpillar into a butterfly, new wings of faith emerge from a new nature, and the regenerate man takes flight! God gives the powerless sinner the very ability to do what He requires. When Jesus said to the paralytic man, "Arise, take up your bed, and go to your house" (Matthew 9:6), the man had no ability to follow the Lord's instructions. But along with the command to get up came the gift of healing and strength, enabling him to do what the Lord had said.[17]

The gospel is zealous to give God all the credit for salvation. It strips away every pretense of human achievement until, at last, there is nothing to boast of save Christ alone. In the wake of grace lies slain all competitors for His glory. Regeneration comes first—it is God's initiative; your choosing Christ comes after and only as a result of that prior awakening. Getting that order right will put the glory where it belongs.

## Regeneration Is God's Choice

In that late-night interview with Nicodemus, Jesus likens the mysterious operation of God in the new birth to the wind: "The wind blows where it wishes, and you hear the sound of it, but cannot tell where it comes from and where it goes. So is everyone who is born of the Spirit" (John 3:8). Lost in translation is a little play on words. In the Greek language, the word for "wind" and "Spirit" is the same—*pneuma*. Like the wind, regeneration is mysterious and unpredictable. No one commands it, and no one directs its course. It blows wherever it pleases. It is the sovereign choice of God to decide on whom this wind of mercy will blow, and so it follows His divine initiative.

God brought Ezekiel to a valley of dry bones and asked the prophet, "Can these bones live?" Ezekiel was wise enough to know when not to offer his feeble opinion and replied, "Sovereign LORD, you alone know" (Ezekiel 37:3 NIV). Ezekiel understood whose prerogative it would be for the wind of life to blow over that valley. He knew it was the sovereign choice of God alone. God views fallen humanity as a cemetery of corpses, like that valley of dry bones, and "gives life to . . . whom He will" (John 5:21). Some, He passes over and leaves to their sinful inclinations. But for others, He chooses to call forth the breath of life to "breathe on these slain, that they may live" (Ezekiel 37:9). Our calling and mandate as the church is to give the gospel invitation indiscriminately to all. But to the question of whom the wind will fall upon, we can only reply, "Sovereign LORD, you alone know."

I have often tried to predict which way the wind will blow. I thought that so-and-so would be saved because I imagined I could see the leaves rustling. And if it were up to me to choose the direction of the wind, it would certainly be on *this one*, Lord—why just look at all the wonderful qualities they would bring to the kingdom! Like a spiritual weatherman, I thought I could forecast the direction of God's mercy, only to see the so-called likely candidate for salvation turn away from Christ and another (whom I never thought would repent) bow the knee in faith. When I observe such distinguishing grace, I am both humbled and struck with reverent fear. Even among the two thieves that flanked Golgotha, upon only one did the wind blow. Both men needed repentance. Both suffered the same pain and saw the same Lord dying beside him. Yet only one believed. How do we account for the difference? Surely both men would be swept up in the wind of mercy being so close in proximity to the Lord as He was even in the midst of His passion. "[But] one thief was saved that no sinner might despair—but only one, that no sinner might presume."[18] The wind blows where it wishes.

# CHAPTER 4

# OF MICE, MEN & GOD

Lennie drummed on the table with his fingers.

"George?"

"Huh?"

"George, how long's it gonna be till we get that little place an' live on the fatta the lan'—an' rabbits?"

"I don't know," said George. "We gotta get a big stake together. I know a little place we can get cheap, but they ain't givin' it away."

Old Candy turned slowly over. His eyes were wide open. He watched George carefully.

Lennie said, "Tell about that place, George."

"I jus' tol' you, jus' las' night."

"Go on—tell again, George."

"Well, it's ten acres," said George. "Got a little win'mill. Got a little shack on it, an' a chicken run. Got a kitchen, orchard, cherries, apples, peaches, 'cots, nuts, got a few berries. They's a place for alfalfa and plenty water to flood it. They's a pig pen—"

"An' rabbits, George."[19]

In John Steinbeck's novel *Of Mice and Men*, George, his dim-witted friend Lennie, and an old man named Candy dream out loud of the day they would buy their own little piece of heaven—a tiny farm where they could throw off the shackles of a boss and be masters of the universe. George was the mastermind of the plan. When it dawned on him that the combination of all their savings along with a few more months of work might actually make this dream come true, he could hardly believe it. "They fell into a silence. They looked at one another, amazed. This thing they had never really believed in was coming true."[20]

But tragically, George's plan would never come to pass. The unintended foolishness of Lennie and a thousand other circumstances would be his undoing. George's plan failed because, like the best-laid plans of mice and men, his plan was fallible. Of course, he could not see the future, and he could not anticipate unforeseen circumstances—a bad combination as far as plans go. But there was something else at play. In addition to his ignorance of what lay ahead, his desired outcome was vulnerable to the choices that *other* people would make.

Is that the way it works with the plans of God? Through the mouth of the prophet, God declares, "My counsel shall stand, and I will do all My pleasure" (Isaiah 46:10). Unlike the plans of men, God proclaims His plans to be unshakable and unstoppable: "Many are the plans in the mind of a man, but it is the purpose of the LORD that will stand (Proverbs 19:21 ESV). To be sure, God has a great advantage over us in plan making because He knows the future.

So then, is that all there is to it? Is this future knowledge the thing that ensures the outcome of God's plans? Does He simply look ahead to see which way His creatures will go and then plan accordingly? If so, that would make God a dependent being. His divine will would be contingent on the will of the creation! Right now, as you read this sentence, billions of creature choices are taking place. Countless decisions of humans, angels, and demons are going on right now, from the mundane to the profound. Somewhere, someone is deciding what to eat for lunch, while in another place, leaders are making decisions that will lead to armies in conflict. Each of the myriad of choices going on at every moment has the potential to change the course of lives, families, and nations. If God is not in control of billions of creature choices, then He cannot say with certainty, "I will do *all* My pleasure." If God is either ignorant or unable to direct the multitude of decisions that happen every single day, then He is not God, and we can have no confidence that His plans will succeed. Such a God is forever reacting to the whims of His creation—going with the flow and tailoring His plans to fit our decisions. Far from doing all His pleasure, God would be forced to conform His plan to the best available option left to Him in the end!

Thankfully, the Scriptures do not describe God's plans as if they are hanging on the decisions of men. Psalm 33:10–11 states, "The LORD brings the counsel of the nations to nothing; He makes the plans of the peoples of no effect. The counsel of the LORD stands forever, the plans of His heart to all generations." God has no need to modify His goals in response to our decisions. Proverbs 21:1 says, "The king's heart is in the hand of the LORD, like the rivers of water; He turns it wherever He wishes." God can say with omnipotent confidence that He will do all His pleasure because He rules and reigns over every free decision that is made in the universe. Not one thought rises or falls apart from His decree.

Consider, for example, God's plan for Saul of Tarsus. Saul was a persecutor of the early church and made it his ambition to wipe out the followers of Jesus. But God had a different agenda for Saul's life. On the road to Damascus, He knocked Saul off his horse and gave him his new marching orders as Paul the apostle to the gentiles. At that moment on the road, there was an intersection of wills. God's plan for Paul's life collided headlong with Paul's plans. God won the contest, of course, but how so? Did the Sovereign simply invoke a divine veto and overrule Paul's will with His? Did Paul freely choose Christ as his Lord and Savior? Of course he did! In the blinding light of Christ, he asked, "Who are You, Lord?" (Acts 9:5). Wrapped up in that one little word, "Lord," was a heart bursting with repentance, faith, and surrender to King Jesus. And yet still, in the light of his freely made decision to kneel to Christ, look how Paul later described his conversion:

> I advanced in Judaism beyond many of my contemporaries in my own nation, being more exceedingly zealous for the traditions of my fathers. But . . . it pleased God, who *separated me from my mother's womb* and called me through His grace, to reveal His Son in me. (Galatians 1:14–16)

Paul declares that God had planned his conversion to Christ and had set him apart from *the womb* for His purposes. When God said from all eternity, "My counsel shall stand, and I will do all My pleasure," one of those pleasures was to elect Paul as the apostle to the gentiles. But in the light of Paul's freedom of choice, how could God make such advanced plans for his life? It would be nice if Paul's decisions just happened to line up with God's pleasure, but couldn't it have gone either way? Did God look ahead to see what Paul would decide that day on the road to Damascus and then adjust His plan accordingly? That is not how the Scripture describes it. The Sovereign God set Paul aside in the womb to conform to His plans. Certainly, Paul's choices were included in that design, but God's plans were not contingent on what Paul would do. Quite the opposite—Paul's life was contingent on God's pleasure! Paul would later tell the Ephesians he was no special case and that God has similarly planned the destiny of every believer:

> In Him also we have obtained an inheritance, being predestined according to the purpose of Him who works all things according to the counsel of His will. (Ephesians 1:11)

Ah, there is that word again. If you recall, it came up back in chapter 1, and we can't put it off any longer—"predestination," the word that has launched a thousand theological conversations and caused so much controversy. Many would rather it did not exist. Yet there it is in our Bibles for us to reckon with. If we believe the Bible to be God's word, then "predestination" is a word from God. It is a word that we must come to know if we are to know the God who reveals Himself in sacred writ.

The prefix "pre-" in "predestination" sends a grammar signal that this is something that happens before. Before what? Before the arrival of a certain destination; thus, we have "*pre*destination." In salvific terms, there are only two destinations beyond this life: heaven and hell. So then predestination has to do with our *ultimate* destination.[21] God had planned the final destination of the elect before they even began the journey. Before the world was made, every one of the sheep was foreknown, foreloved, and destined by God for the sheepfold.

Predestination is a simple as this: God had a plan. Long before God said, “Let there be,” there was a blueprint in mind. Before He made the stars, planets, or a single dandelion, He had a design in place. And now, the Sovereign God is working out that plan to completion. Would you expect anything different? Would you even want a God who didn't have a plan but was sort of making it up as He goes along? It is no surprise that the God of infinite wisdom had an end in mind before He began. Any thinking being makes a plan before acting. It may be a foolish plan. It may be a hasty plan. But regardless of why the chicken decided to cross the road, even its bird brain made a plan to get to the other side.

When I was a boy in the Scouts, they handed me a bar of Ivory soap because we were going to make soap carvings. I liked this idea, so I eagerly began carving. My buddy asked me, “What are you making?” “I dunno yet,” I replied. Ten minutes later, he asked again. “I still don't know yet,” I said. Twenty minutes later, I had nothing left but a pile of soap chips. However, I had learned a valuable lesson—an artist should have some design in mind before he begins. Of course, God had a plan before He started! It is self-evident to the nature of God that He had a prior design in mind as to how it would all turn out. But unlike the plans of mice and men, the plans of God are being worked out with sovereign, omnipotent perfection. And swept up into that plan are a chosen people for salvation who can rest in the knowledge that God will accomplish His purposes. Why? Because they are chosen "according to the purpose of Him who works all things according to the counsel of His will." I take the meaning of *all things* to include—well, all things, even the free choices of men. God's plans cannot be thwarted (Job 42:2) because they are not contingent on anything except His divine pleasure.

In Romans 9, the apostle Paul draws on a story from the Old Testament to teach us how God's election plan works. In chapter 25 of Genesis, we find Isaac's wife, Rebekah, to be pregnant with twin boys. Now, it was the tradition that the firstborn son would receive the lion's share of the inheritance, and the other siblings would be subservient to him. But God had a different plan, which defied the customs of men. He chose to bless the younger son instead. Paul explains in Romans 9:9–13:

> For this is the word of promise: "At this time I will come and Sarah shall have a son." And not only this, but when Rebecca also had conceived by one man, even by our father Isaac (for the children not yet being born, nor having done any good or evil, that the purpose of God according to election might stand, not of works but of Him who calls), it was said to her, "The older shall serve the younger." As it is written, "Jacob I have loved, but Esau I have hated."

Divine election in salvation is clearly the subject of this passage. Paul states explicitly, "That the purpose of God according to election might stand." Well, what is this purpose? What is the bedrock message that God is sending through election? "Not of works but of Him who calls." God's choice in election destroys any human contribution in salvation and makes it entirely a result of God's gracious calling. The plans of men designed the blessing to fall on Esau, but the sovereign plan trumped all. In choosing Jacob, "God aims to undermine any attempt to limit His freedom in election."[22]

Some try to escape the force of this passage by reducing God's choice to nations. But aside from the fact that individuals are clearly being addressed here ("*Jacob* I have loved, but *Esau* I have hated"), what does such a maneuver accomplish? What are nations made of, if not individuals? I will address this objection with more detail in chapter 5, but for now, let us come to terms with the reality that, regardless of what they might represent, Jacob and Esau were individual men. And God chose to bless one man while passing over the other.

The fact that the apostle chose a pair of twin brothers for his "exhibit A" of election is no coincidence. What better example to illustrate God's sovereign choice than twins? In the case of these brothers, every human element that might influence God one way or the other is removed. We cannot say it was upbringing that made the difference or their environment or their genes. Everything is identical down to the same womb! One is loved by God, and the other is despised, yet there is not a single factor we can point to in them that provoked either response. In fact, Paul points out that God made His choice to favor Jacob over Esau while they were still as yet unborn. We might assume that God loved Jacob more because he was faithful or obedient. But such is not the case. Jacob was a jerk. He stole his brother's birthright and lied to his father in order to cheat Esau out of his inheritance. Jacob's very name means "deceiver." Both Jacob and Esau had exactly the same claim on God's grace—none! The flesh desperately wants to find something in the record of these men that can explain God's choice. But they were "not yet born." They had not done "any good or evil." The whole point is that election is not a reward for merit because the decision was made before any merit was possible.

The divine initiative is taken in absolute freedom. God is not boxed in so that He must choose anyone. He is free. And within that perfect freedom of God, the chosen find an unrestricted, unfettered, unconditional love—a love that defies any reason found in them.

The ultimate reason God chooses to love Jacob (or any of the elect) is for "the praise of the glory of His grace" (Ephesians 1:6). But as to why God elects each individual to the number of the redeemed is not revealed in Scripture. "The secret things belong to the

LORD our God" (Deuteronomy 29:29). God is under no obligation to tell us the "why" behind *anything* He does, much less everything He does. In His wisdom, He has chosen to keep that particular piece of information within His divine heart. Perhaps He will reveal it in glory, but for now, we must be content with His silence. People often object that God is random or flippant here—as if He were drawing names out of a hat. But just because God does not tell us His reason gives us no right to conclude there isn't one. If there is anything we know about the God of the Bible, it's that there is reason and purpose behind all that He does and all that He does is good. The Great Shepherd has a reason behind the choice of each one of His sheep, and we can be sure of this: it is a holy reason, a perfect reason, and for now, an unknown reason to us.

But though you cannot know the reason why God chose you individually, you can know from Romans 9:9–13 what the reason *is not*. It is not because of anything found in you. God loved Jacob before he had done anything (anything past, anything present, anything future)—which means God's love was not because of Jacob's righteous record. It was not because he was better than Esau. It was not because of his future potential. It was not because God looked ahead, saw Jacob's love, and responded in kind. It was not because he qualified for that love. God loved him just because He loved him. He loved him for reasons found only in Himself.

Christian, in order that the purpose of God according to election might stand, not of works but of Him who calls, God loved you. There was nothing you did or would ever do to provoke His affection. Love was His plan long before you had any possible opportunity to either bless it or blow it. Please, dear reader, don't miss the love because you can't get past the mystery! I understand that God's election is a hard thing to get your mind around. It requires hard thinking, careful study, good-faith questions, and examination of the Scriptures. I encourage you to do all of that. But along the way, remember, God did not reveal this truth just to give us an intellectual exercise to ponder. He wants us to drink deeply from the well of His love. Please don't go on forever, debating, thinking, and analyzing so that you miss the love. Dear chosen of God, hear Him singing over you, "I have loved you with an everlasting love" (Jeremiah 31:3).

The best-laid plans of mice and men may fail, but the plans of the Lord stand firm forever. If anything happens in the universe, if one sparrow falls to the ground, we can be sure it is on the divine blueprint. And if He plans all the lesser things, then of course He plans the greatest thing—the salvation of His people. One fine day He will roll up His plans, and having completed all His purposes, He will say to His elect, "Come, you blessed of My Father, inherit the kingdom prepared for you from the foundation of the world" (Matthew 25:34).

# CHAPTER 5

# OBJECTIONS

Though the life hidden in Christ began for me as a hand raised at a youth retreat, for many years I was unaware of God's divine initiative in my salvation. I have since discovered that this truth has been believed and confessed by Christians for two millennia, but the churches I grew up in did not. Consequently, upon my first exposure to these things, I was shocked, I was surprised, and I didn't like it. I had many questions and objections that (to me, anyway) seemed insurmountable.

My first reaction was to turn away from this. But though my flesh wanted to run, my heart could not escape the weight of Scripture undergirding this truth. The longer I searched, the more it became evident that the Bible is saturated with this teaching—indicating that this is more than some secondary issue I could opt out of if it didn't suit me. There is something fundamental here to the gospel itself that I had not seen. I couldn't put it all together yet, but I could sense an emerging truth meant to be savored and cherished. I was drawn back to the search, and eventually, I came to realize that my objections were not so airtight as I had once thought.

One by one, as my arguments lay slain before God's Word, it dawned on me—it is all true. God really loves me like this. God has chosen me. I had already tasted God's love in Christ, but now a whole new sweetness burst upon my tongue. A depth of love I had scarcely imagined came into view. I can only describe my experience as like being saved all over again.

Perhaps you are as I once was. You are reading these concepts for the first time, and the whole thing doesn't sit well. Many objections and questions are rising in your mind, and you are tempted to close this book and not think about these things anymore. But you have come this far, and for that, I thank you. I ask you to please hear me out just a little longer. You may be on guard, with your defenses up. You are not interested in a theological hair-splitting exercise—you just love Jesus. Me too! But I have some genuine concerns that are too important to ignore. I also have a beautiful truth that must be proclaimed. So, I plead with you to allow me to speak as a brother, as iron sharpening iron. Allow me to present to you in this chapter some of the most common objections to the divine initiative, along with some hopefully helpful responses.

# OBJECTION #1

## It's Not Fair!

By far, the number one objection that arises to God's divine initiative is "This is not fair!" When we hear of God choosing some and passing over others, our democratic sense of fair play kicks in, and we cry foul. I would like to answer that objection by first distinguishing between fairness and justice.

Is election just? That's the real question that lies behind the objection of unfairness. But fairness and justice are not the same things. Fairness means that everyone receives equal treatment. Justice, on the other hand, is to receive *what you are owed*. Justice is what you deserve. Certainly, there are many times when justice demands equal treatment. For example, if a woman receives less pay than a man for the same work, we would say it is unjust because she was not treated equally. But fairness and justice are not inseparably linked. If a store decides to promote sales by giving out random prizes to its customers, that is not unjust—even though all the customers were not treated the same. It was not fair (equal). Some received prizes while others did not. Notice that the key difference between the unequal prizes and the unequal wages is that which is owed. The woman is owed equal pay for equal work because she earned it. Inequality, in this case, brings about injustice because she is being deprived of that which rightfully belongs to her. In the second example, however, inequality of prizes is not unjust because the store did not owe a prize to any of its customers. Those shoppers who did not receive a prize had not been deprived of anything.

So, concerning fairness, does God treat everyone the same? The biblical answer is a decided no! God revealed Himself to Moses at the burning bush, but He did not reveal Himself to Pharaoh. God gave the law to the nation of Israel, but to the Hittite nation, no such revelation was bestowed. During a famine, one widow's meal barrel miraculously replenished while many other widows received no such provision. The resurrected Jesus appeared to Saul of Tarsus, but He did not appear to Herod.[23] Such examples of God treating people differently abound in Scripture. This inequality is not a divine embarrassment hidden within the margins of Scripture. Jesus openly points it out: "And many lepers were in Israel in the time of Elisha the prophet, and none of them was cleansed except Naaman the Syrian" (Luke 4:27).

Clearly, in the economy of God, grace and mercy are not equally distributed. It is not a *fair* distribution. But is it unjust? That is the real question before us. Does this unequal allotment of God's favor amount to a violation of that which is morally right? God answers:

> "I will have mercy on whomever I will have mercy, and I will have compassion on whomever I will have compassion." (Romans 9:15)

God replies to this shadow of doubt that has been cast upon His justice and integrity by informing the creature that it is His divine prerogative to dispense mercy in any way He chooses. In saying this, God gives us a grand principle of how mercy works: *mercy is owed to none.*[24]

Inequality only becomes unjust when someone is deprived of that which rightfully belongs to him. But to whom does mercy belong? Mercy is to forebear just punishment. Mercy is kindness extended to one who rightfully deserves judgment. It is to withhold the penalty that has been earned. No one owns the right to mercy except the mercy giver. When people receive mercy, they are receiving the opposite of what is due them—wrath. God never owes mercy to anyone because mercy is, by definition, never owed.

Imagine ten men sentenced to the gallows. Each man is guilty of a heinous crime and has earned the just penalty that is now about to be executed. Each neck is fitted with a noose. Last words are said. The executioner looks at his watch as the final seconds are ticking down. But just before the clock strikes, a messenger bursts out the news, "The governor has pardoned two of the men!" The rope is removed from two very relieved prisoners, who are then set free. Is the governor now obligated to spare them all since he showed mercy to some? Not at all. The rest of the condemned men are guilty and are receiving exactly what they deserve. Two men received mercy, the remaining eight received justice, but none of them received injustice.

But the common complaint is that election sure *seems* like an injustice. I cannot help but notice that this is the same objection that the apostle Paul anticipates will be raised to sovereign election: "What shall we say then? Is there unrighteousness with God?" (Romans 9:14). I wish I had a dollar for every time someone cast an accusation at the justice of God in response to the teaching of the divine initiative. Now let me ask you an honest question. Would your understanding of salvation ever cause someone to raise the Romans 9:14 objection? Would anyone ever question the righteousness of God after hearing your explanation of the gospel? Paul's understanding of the gospel *did* anticipate that accusation. And I count myself in good company when I hear the same complaint because I strongly suspect it means we are saying the same thing.

To think that justice demands an equal dispensation of God's mercy is to misunderstand the very meaning of mercy. Such thinking also underestimates how hell-deserving we really are. When God looks at humanity, He does not see a world filled with good people deserving His favor. He sees a race of rebels that have universally trampled His glory. God would be entirely just to wipe the human race from the face of the earth. God will have mercy *on whomever He will have mercy.* Which guilty people and how many guilty people He pardons is completely within His sovereign discretion. He could show mercy to some—or to none—and not one of us could look up from our guilty record and lay a charge of injustice before the Judge of all the earth. If it amazes us that God does not show mercy to everyone, then we have misplaced our amazement. When we consider the magnitude of our offense before Him, the true wonder is why God is merciful to anyone at all.

# OBJECTION #2

## Divine Sovereignty Is Incompatible with Human Freedom

"The secret things belong to the LORD our God," declares Deuteronomy 29:29. God is under no more obligation to explain Himself to His creatures than a father is bound to justify his ways to a four-year-old daughter. God has chosen not to reveal to us many things, and one of them is the mystery of divine sovereignty and human freedom. How can God plan and purpose everything that is going to happen without, at the same time, destroying man's ability to make real choices? A predestinating God who "[declares] the end from the beginning" (Isaiah 46:10) seems at total odds with the Savior's plea: "If anyone thirsts, let him come to Me and drink" (John 7:37). For many people, this is an intellectual bridge that cannot be crossed. For them, divine sovereignty and free will are incompatible—true freedom of choice cannot exist side by side with a God who has already determined the outcome of everything. Such an arrangement, it is supposed, would make us nothing more than marionettes and God the cosmic puppeteer.

But we must not make the mistake of assuming that since *we* can't figure out how these two things go together neither can God. Scripture is full of passages that proclaim the truth of God sovereignly determining all things. The Bible also plainly declares that we have free choice. The fact that God does not reveal how these truths coexist does not mean there *is* no explanation or that they cannot be reconciled. In placing these truths side by side in His Word, God is demonstrating that they do harmonize.

In Proverbs 16:9, we see just one of many examples where the Bible presents human freedom alongside divine sovereignty: "A man's heart plans his way, but the LORD directs his steps." We find in this passage two ideas that do not seem to go together, and yet here they are in the same inspired sentence.

| **Divine Sovereignty and Human Freedom Together in Proverbs 16:9** | |
|---|---|
| **Man Is Free** | **God Is Sovereign** |
| A man's heart plans his way | but the LORD directs his steps |

We have been endowed by our Maker with the ability to choose our own path: a man's heart plans his way. The decisions we make are real and free. And yet, simultaneously, God determines every step we take: but the LORD directs his steps. God does not explain how these things coherently merge, nor is He obliged to do so. We, on the other hand, are obliged to take Him at His word. Consider the following examples of God's sovereignty and human freedom appearing simultaneously on the pages of holy Scripture:

| Man Is Free | God Is Sovereign |
|---|---|
| "Choose for yourselves this day whom you will serve." Joshua 24:15 | "The king's heart is in the hand of the LORD, like the rivers of water; He turns it wherever He wishes." Proverbs 21:1 |
| "If you confess with your mouth the Lord Jesus and believe in your heart that God raised Him from the dead, you will be saved." Romans 10:9 | "Both Herod and Pontius Pilate . . . were gathered together to do whatever Your hand and Your purpose determined before to be done." Acts 4:27–28 |
| "Come to Me, all you who labor and are heavy laden, and I will give you rest." Matthew 11:28 | "All that the Father gives Me will come to Me." John 6:37 |
| "I stand at the door and knock. If anyone hears My voice and opens the door, I will come in." Revelation 3:20 | "Whose names are not written in the Book of Life from the foundation of the world." Revelation 17:8 |

Both sides of this table are equally the Word of God. Though they may *seem* contradictory, either column contains Holy Spirit-inspired truth that is to be believed. But can we talk honestly from the heart? Which column of passages do you like? What I mean is, which set of Scriptures fit more readily into your usual way of thinking? Which column makes you uncomfortable? It is naive to think that we come to the Scriptures emotionally neutral. But one's discomfort with the column on the right or left has no bearing on the truth of it. As Christians committed to the whole Word of God, we are obligated to believe, embrace, proclaim, rejoice in, and celebrate the truth revealed in both columns.

"But I can't make these two columns gel" is the common complaint. So what? The fact that you and I can't work it out proves nothing except that we do not have the mind of God. If God places human freedom alongside His sovereign plans and actions, then it is plain that this poses no contradiction in the mind of God. We all like things to make sense. And so our tendency is to emphasize Scriptures that fit neatly into the framework of our thinking and minimize passages that complicate that picture. In doing this, we miss wonderful truths God is proclaiming and, at the same time, destroy the truth we think we are protecting. The wise course is to just let God be God. Those portions of God's Word that we cannot intellectually bring together (due to the limits of our finite minds), we must hold in tension by faith in the One who is speaking.

Many concepts in Scripture require the faithful to believe what they cannot entirely comprehend. The nature of the Trinity, that God has no beginning, and that evil entered God's good universe without Him being the author of it are among the many paradoxes God has declared to be true. Though we cannot fully comprehend these things, we *apprehend* them by faith. That which is presently a mystery we embrace as truth—trusting such mysteries to be resolved in the divine mind.

When it comes to human freedom and divine sovereignty, the temptation is to throw out (or minimize) the latter in order to protect free will. But the task of the believer is to *believe* God! God's Word teaches that you are free and your choices are real. God's Word also teaches that He has determined whatsoever comes to pass. We must bow before both realities and leave the mystery in His hands.

# OBJECTION #3

## Doesn't God Choose Everybody?

Election raises some tough questions to which the Bible gives good, satisfying answers. But coming to grips with what Scripture has to say on this subject requires careful study, prayer, and much contemplation. One way to quickly bypass the whole issue is simply to say, "God chooses everybody." Simple and done! With one stroke, this statement eliminates any need to work through the implications of election. God simply elected everybody.

What does it mean to choose? It is to make a selection out of the alternatives available. To choose is to prefer one option over another. To choose everything is to make the word meaningless because choosing is, by definition, a distinct selection out of the many. It is not possible to choose, unless at the same time something is passed over. If nothing is passed over—if nothing is preferred—then nothing is chosen. Let's look at the word "chosen" as it appears elsewhere in the Bible:

➢ **"When it was day, He called His disciples to Himself; and from them He *chose* twelve" (Luke 6:13).** At one point, Jesus had at least seventy disciples (Luke 10:1). Jesus made a deliberate choice of twelve men for a special purpose, passing over the rest. A selection of a few was made from the many.

➢ **"Many are called, but few are *chosen*" (Matthew 22:14).** The gospel invitation goes out to the whole world. But Jesus tells us here that from the many who are called or invited, few are chosen. A selection of the few out of the many is taking place.

➢ **"I do not speak concerning all of you. I know whom I have *chosen*" (John 13:18).** Jesus (speaking of Judas Iscariot) plainly states that He is not choosing everybody. His choice is a selection of some out of the total options available.

➢ **"You are not of the world, but I have *chosen* you out of the world" (John 15:19).** The Lord says that His disciples are chosen out of the world. He does not choose everybody, but out of the whole world, Jesus has selected some.

When the Bible says in Ephesians 1:4 that "[God] *chose* us in Him," it is clear from the use of "chose" in other passages that God is not choosing everybody. Rather, He is making a particular selection of some from the many. And that is the whole point! Paul was not singing praises to God because He treated us all the same. He is celebrating the incredible reality that, though we should have been condemned like the rest, we were selected as targets of God's mercy. Election is meant to both humble and encourage the believer. It humbles us when we realize that God's choice was entirely gracious and undeserved. We have nothing to boast of, for the distinguishing difference between us and the non-elect is grace alone. But election also encourages because it reminds us of the enduring, special love God has for His people and the great lengths He went to make us His own. When all seems out of control, the believer can soar with the thought, "I am specially loved by an electing God. He made a particular choice to save me, and that means He will never let me go."

# OBJECTION #4

## Inability Destroys Culpability

The case has been made in this book for the divine initiative of God in salvation. God had to make the first move precisely because we could not. The fallen nature so damaged our mind and will as to render us morally incapable of turning to Christ. The sinner—apart from divine intervention—has not the spiritual ability to change his sinful nature, turn from sin, and believe the gospel. Let me remind you from chapter 2 of what the fallen person has no ability to do:

| What the Fallen Person Cannot Do | |
|---|---|
| **Change his nature** | "Can the Ethiopian change his skin or the leopard its spots?" (Jeremiah 13:23) |
| **Understand the things of God** | "The natural man does not receive the things of the Spirit of God, for they are foolishness to him; nor can he know them, for they are spiritually discerned." (1 Corinthians 2:14) |
| **Submit to God's law** | "The carnal mind is enmity against God; for it is not subject to the law of God, nor indeed can be." (Romans 8:7) |
| **Come to Christ** | "No one can come to Me unless it has been granted to him by My Father." (John 6:65) |

How then can we be held responsible for that which we are unable to do? It would seem patently unjust for God to take a person to task for a task they have no ability to perform in the first place. Surely, if the fallen person cannot incline himself to Christ, it would be unthinkable to hold him responsible, much less eternally condemn him, for his failure to comply. And yet Scripture does declare the fallen man powerless to hear the voice of Christ: "Why do you not understand My speech? Because you are *not able* to listen to My word" (John 8:43). Scripture is equally clear that the fallen man will be held responsible for his rejection of Christ: "He who does not believe is condemned already" (John 3:18). How can these things be reconciled?

It is true that inability destroys culpability in most cases. Justice does not hold you responsible for what you cannot do—unless *you* caused the inability. If your actions render you unable to comply with that which is right, you are still responsible for the infraction. This is easy to demonstrate. Just go rack up a huge balance on a credit card that you cannot afford to pay back. Then call up Visa and tell them, "I am incapable of repaying this debt; therefore, you cannot hold me responsible." They will likely disagree with the notion that inability destroys culpability. Or consider a more serious example: A drunk driver veers off the road and injures a pedestrian. The accused stands before the judge and declares, "I am not responsible for this man's injury because I am incapable of driving straight when I am drunk." The judge will then, of course, reply, "You are responsible for your reckless driving because you caused the drunkenness."

When the Scriptures declare us morally unable to turn from sin and respond to the Savior, let us not consider ourselves poor, innocent victims of this condition as if we were born with a spiritual handicap. Do not forget that we caused the condition that damaged our spiritual faculties. We are born blind to Christ's beauty, deaf to His voice, unwilling and unable to turn to Him because of our original sin. God said, "But of the tree of the knowledge of good and evil you shall not eat, for in the day that you eat of it you shall surely die" (Genesis 2:17). All of us (in the perfect representation of Adam) did eat. We are not victims when we are born spiritually dead—we are convicts, bearing the divine sentence that has been justly imposed.

We come into this world spiritually intoxicated. We are completely culpable when we cannot stay on the straight and narrow road because we are driving under the influence of sin. We caused this. In Eden, we recklessly made our choice, and the resulting damage is ours to own. When we cannot hear His voice because of our fallen stupor; we are fully to blame. When He bids us repent and believe on the

Son, it is totally our fault when we find ourselves stubborn and unwilling. It is, therefore, no wonder that God holds us responsible for the moral inability that we ourselves caused. The true wonder is the gospel that overcomes our inability. God calls us to do what we cannot—and then grants what He commands.

# OBJECTION #5

## Election Teaches That God Stops People from Believing

A caricature is a ludicrous exaggeration of defects found in people or things. I wish I could say that is what this objection is. Unfortunately, it does not even rise to the level of caricature. It is, rather, a gross distortion of the divine initiative. And yet, this accusation is made frequently.

After I taught a class on this subject, one dear sister approached me afterward, clearly disturbed by what she had just heard. She proclaimed, "You are saying that God keeps people out of heaven who want Jesus!" As a preacher, I am aware that each time I speak, three sermons get delivered: the one I thought I preached, the one that actually came out of my mouth, and the one that people heard. Yet, still, I couldn't help but be bewildered as to how this woman managed to hear *that* from what I had just said. You couldn't get me to say that with a gun to my head! So then let me state as clearly as I can: You must repent and believe on Christ to be saved; and all who repent and believe on Christ will be saved. The question is: Who will want to do that?

To have saving faith is to see the value and beauty of God in His Son, Jesus Christ. The fallen man is unable to see this—not because God is preventing him from looking but because he prefers to set his gaze upon his own worth and beauty instead. You cannot value God above all and, at the same time, value self above all. God is not preventing the non-elect from wanting Christ. They do that freely on their own, and God simply gives them what they desire.

The most severe judgment is for God to give the sinner what he wants. The apostle Paul puts it like this: "And even as they did not like to retain God in their knowledge, God *gave them over* to a debased mind" (Romans 1:28). God does not inject unbelief into the non-elect; He simply lets the wicked be wicked still (Revelation 22:11).

"I will harden Pharaoh's heart," declares the Lord in Exodus 7:3. What exactly did God do to accomplish this hardening? Nothing. God left Pharaoh to his own wicked inclinations. It is not necessary to create unbelief in the heart of the sinner—it is already present, and if simply left alone, it will harden and calcify. If God were to lift His restraining, keeping hand from any one of us, we would all become stone. That is a huge difference from how God works in election. In election, God is active. He intervenes. He gives a new heart. He resurrects. He gives faith. But to the non-elect, God is entirely passive. He is not stopping the sinner from coming to Christ but simply lets them be. What could be fairer than for God to give you what you want?

Consider this fictional conversation between God and a non-elect person:

**Non-elect:** "God, it is unfair that you have regenerated the hearts of others but not mine!"

**GOD:** "Do you desire My Son?"

**Non-Elect:** "No."

**GOD:** "Why, then, do you want Me to give you what you do not wish for?"

The elect desire Christ, and they have what they want. The non-elect do not desire Christ, and they have what they want.

# OBJECTION #6

## Election Destroys Evangelism

It is a very discouraging thing to proclaim the good news of Jesus to your lost loved ones only to have it rejected. Yet we muster our courage to try again in the hope that there is some potential that they might one day turn from sin and be saved. But why bother trying if God has already determined who will believe? It would seem that the divine initiative in salvation destroys any motivation for evangelism. Since God has predestined that all His elect will believe and be saved, it appears then that the task of evangelism has been reduced to folding our arms and waiting on God to do His thing. It's hard enough these days to motivate Christians to witness to their family and neighbors. If they believe this, it is supposed, no one will even bother! Just let election take its course. The main problem with this objection is that it's just plain historically false. I need only cite a few names in church history to demonstrate this truth.

| Great Evangelists Who Believed in the Divine Initiative | |
|---|---|
| **William Carey** | Considered the "father of modern missions." Devoted his life to bringing the gospel to India. He founded the Baptist Missionary Society. |
| **George Whitefield** | Itinerant preacher who led a series of revivals known as the "Great Awakening" in which tens of thousands were saved. |
| **Charles Spurgeon** | The "Prince of Preachers," estimated to have preached during his lifetime to ten million people, leading thousands to Christ. |
| **Jonathan Edwards** | Revivalist and theologian. His sermons, such as "Sinners in the Hands of an Angry God," are said to have moved people to open weeping and repentance while he preached. |
| **David Brainerd** | Missionary to the American Indians. It can be argued that his life and testimony (recorded in his diary) has sent more people to the mission field than any other person in history. |

The preceding list reads like an evangelism hall of fame—and this is only to name a few! Each of these men believed and proclaimed the divine initiative; yet who can deny the evangelical zeal that moved them to make such an impact for Christ? These men demonstrate that belief in a predestinating God does not extinguish evangelical fervor. Those who insist that the belief and the practice are incompatible must do so in the face of a contrary historical record. It cannot be denied that individuals who embraced a God who sovereignly determines the number of the redeemed have not only robustly propagated the gospel but have *led the way* in evangelism and missions. But why is that? Why did they evangelize, knowing that God has already chosen who will be saved? Let me offer you three reasons:

**1. Because we are commanded to do so.**

"Go therefore and make disciples of all the nations" (Matthew 28:19). Full stop. The Christian needs no other justification or motivation to evangelize than the command of Christ, in whom all authority rests.

**2. God predestines not only the end but also the means.**

God does not bring the elect to saving faith by waving His hand from heaven; God has ordained that, at some point, each of His elect will hear the gospel and turn to Christ. Evangelism is the *means* by which they hear and believe. "And how shall they believe in

Him of whom they have not heard? And how shall they hear without a preacher?" (Romans 10:14–15). In God's great design to save His elect, He not only predestines that they will believe but also that someone will tell them about Jesus—someone like you! If God ordains a man in India to be saved, He also ordains an Amy Carmichael to go to India with the gospel. God ordains the boat she travels on and plans the very moment the good news passes from her lips to his ears.

In His parable of the sower (Matthew 13:1–9), Jesus teaches us to expect most of the gospel seed we scatter to fall upon the non-elect and bear no fruit (the path, the stony ground, the thorny ground). But Jesus went on to give the encouraging good news that some seed will fall on good soil (the elect) and produce a crop. It is never our job to try and figure out who the elect are. That is God's business. Our task is to throw big handfuls of seed all over the place. Any spot you see in the field—just seed it! Where that seed falls, whether hard ground, thorny ground, or good ground, is up to God. If each of the elect had an *E* tattooed on their forehead, we could stop scattering seed everywhere and witness to them alone. But of course, they don't, and so our job is to "preach the gospel to every creature" (Mark 16:15). We evangelize because that is God's predestined means to produce His predestined end.

**3. God's divine initiative is the only true motivation for evangelism.**

Before I embraced the divine initiative, I once stood in a circle of Christians about to pray. Various prayer requests were spoken. Among them was my own request for prayers to be offered on behalf of a lost loved one. I wanted God to save this person. I have never forgotten the struggle that filled my mind and heart in the moments after those words left my mouth. What exactly was I asking God to do? I wanted Him to bring salvation to my loved one—of that, I was sure. But by praying for God to save her, what active steps was I petitioning God to take? If God was waiting for her to make the first move, then what else could He do but hope she will? Was I praying for God to be really persuasive but ultimately impotent to do anything about her heart? I think every believer who has poured out their soul to God for the salvation of someone dear knows the answer. I was not merely asking God to nudge this person's heart in the right direction. I wanted God to *change* her heart. I was praying for God to remove her heart of stone and give her a heart of flesh. Somehow that prayer request spoke more than I knew—that only God's supernatural power to change her mind, will, and affections was sufficient to transport her out of darkness and into His marvelous light. Dear reader, when you pray for souls to turn to Christ, what exactly are you asking God to do? Are you asking God to *persuade* them or *change* them? It is God's very ability to change hearts that gives us the motive to pray and spread the Word.

I am convinced that evangelism is totally compatible with a belief in the divine initiative. In fact, it is the basis for encouragement in evangelism. Though we have no promise that every gospel venture will succeed, we do have the promise that all the elect will be redeemed. There is "good ground," and some seeds will fall on it to produce a harvest. All that the Father has given to the Son *will come* to the Son (John 6:37). What an encouragement to sow the good news!

Imagine God appearing to a farmer with this message: "Your crop this year is guaranteed." What do you think the farmer will do in response to that assurance? Will he sit back in his recliner, saying, "Why plant at all this year? I can take it easy. It's all been predestined, so why bother?" Quite the opposite! He will bolt out the door and plant as fast as he can. He will plant the upper field that he gave up on long ago because the soil is poor and rocky. He will spend all that he has to buy more seed to plant the ditches and the paths around the farm. He will even expand, entering into contracts with other farmers to plant their fields too. The guaranteed harvest does not discourage him from planting—it fills him with zeal to work harder, go further, and take more risks than he ever would dare before.

I have been blessed by God to have the privilege of participating in the planting of a new church. Prior to that experience, I understood that the heart of the lost person is hard. I knew that theologically. But I didn't *really* know it until I came face-to-face with the wall of unbelief that one encounters in regular attempts at evangelism. Having looked directly into the eyes of so much spiritual callousness, I am convinced more than ever of the deadness of sin. Any church planter will tell you that such a venture is rife with landmines, disappointments, fears within, and conflicts without. Such is the trial of it that if I were pinning my hopes on dead sinners, resurrecting themselves to faith in Christ, I would hang it up today. If it were resting on my cleverness to persuade and the ability of a corpse to hear, I would cease to evangelize forever. For such an endeavor would be a fool's errand that could never succeed. But I continue to scatter the seed with joy because my hope rests in a predestinating God who has guaranteed the harvest. I have been blessed along the way to see some seed take root and spring up to new life in Christ. I am encouraged to keep planting because I know that many divine appointments have been made long before I was born to connect the seed I scatter with soil made ready by the Master. The divine initiative of God, raising His elect from the dead without fail, is the hope of every gospel sower.

# OBJECTION #7

## This Is Fatalism

Fatalism is the philosophy of inevitability. It is the idea that everything that is going to happen will happen and we are powerless to do anything about it. Sometimes folks confuse the divine initiative with fatalism. If one is elect or non-elect, that is your "fate," they say, and so it doesn't matter what you do or don't do. It seems like election is a destiny that will take place regardless of your choices. But the doctrine of God's sovereign election is far from fatalism for the following two reasons:

**1. Fatalism is blind.**

There is no mind behind fatalism. It is a belief that the unthinking mechanical cogs and gears of the universe will produce a certain outcome that cannot be overcome by human resistance. There is no plan or reason behind the idea of fatalism—it is merely the blind forces of the cosmos. Biblical predestination, on the other hand, is the thinking, loving plan of a rational God who is bringing all things under the headship of Christ (Ephesians 1:10). Whereas fatalism produces a meaningless end, the divine initiative is creating a glorious destiny full of purpose and beauty.

**2. Fatalism is in spite of your choices.**

Fatalism supposes a destiny that will take place regardless of your actions or decisions—so it doesn't matter what you choose. But predestination is not in spite of your choices; it is *through* your choices. God has predestined that all His elect will be saved. He has also predestined that all the elect will believe on the Son. Your choice of Christ not only matters, it matters eternally. At the end of history, every soul who trusts in Christ will be saved. Those who neglect this great plan of salvation will perish. And in the mystery of God's sovereign purposes, He has worked the freewill choices of men into His predestined plan. Your choice matters!

# OBJECTION #8

## Election Removes the Hope for My Loved One to Be Saved

I was sitting around a table discussing the divine initiative with a group of Christians. This teaching was new to the small group of men and women posing honest questions and objections to me. One man had a troubled look on his face as the conversation continued. I learned of his adult son, who was not a believer. Based on the father's description, the son was living an openly sinful lifestyle. The man objected, "If election is true, then I have no hope that my son will be saved."

In compiling this chapter on objections, I drew from countless discussions like this one to try and address the most common concerns people have raised to me through the years. This man's objection was from the heart. He was not interested in debating a theological position. He just loved his son and wanted him to be saved. I understand and take his anxiety for his son's soul very seriously. I know that the sheep and the goats are not just faceless numbers to the right and left of Christ. The sheep and the goats have names. I, too, have loved ones that are outside the safety of the cross, and I want to see them come to Christ. My hope for their salvation is not destroyed by sovereign election. In fact, God's sovereign initiative in salvation is my only hope that they will be saved.

This man correctly understood that the only way our unsaved loved ones will turn from sin and choose Christ is if God elects to regenerate their hearts. So he figured, "My son lives an openly sinful lifestyle and therefore must not be among the elect. If that is true," he reasoned, "then there is no hope for him to be saved."

His objection is rooted in the false belief that it is possible to observe a person's lifestyle and determine if they are among God's elect. But this confuses the difference between election and justification. Election occurs unconditionally in eternity past. Justification, on the other hand, takes place in time when the sinner exercises faith in Christ. One's status as a justified person can be observed by the presence of a sanctified life. The fruits of the Spirit sprout up in redeemed hearts. Though our good works do not save us, justification demonstrates itself in a lifestyle of increasing godliness. The apostle John teaches,

> Whoever has been born of God does not sin, for His seed remains in him; and he cannot sin, because he has been born of God. In this the children of God and the children of the devil are manifest: Whoever does not practice righteousness is not of God, nor is he who does not love his brother. (1 John 3:9–10)

John is not teaching that Christians have arrived at a state of flawless moral perfection the moment they are regenerated. If we claim to be without sin, John says, “we deceive ourselves” (1 John 1:8). What is being stated here is that a truly saved person will not continue in patterns of unrepented sin. And so, if someone claims to be saved but lives a lifestyle of gross and ongoing unrepentant sin, it is evidence that they are not born of God. We can readily observe, both in our own lives and in the lives of others, the evidence of justification.

Election, on the other hand, takes place before we are born and is unconditional. It is not based on how we live or anything we do, but rather it is based on God’s grace. There is no observable evidence that someone is elect until that point when they believe on Christ. It matters not how moral or wicked an unbeliever is; an elect person may (and often does) live for years in outright rebellion to God before they are regenerated and turn to Christ. There is no way to know based on a person’s behavior whether God has a divine appointment with them in the future.

| ELECTION | JUSTIFICATION |
|---|---|
| Takes place in eternity past | Takes place in time when a person believes |
| Unconditional | Conditioned on faith and repentance in Christ |
| Displays no evidence prior to conversion | Displays the evidence of sanctification |

I suppose if I had lived in the first century and personally knew the thief who died next to Jesus, I might have guessed he was not among the elect. No doubt I would have cited the years of godless and wicked behavior this man reveled in as evidence of his place among the reprobate. I would have been wrong. For unbeknown to me and unobservable to me, God had an eternal appointment with this man, just hours before he died, to bring him to saving faith.

Concerning the salvation of our loved ones, where then should we place our hope? Do we prefer to hope in dead sinners, resurrecting themselves to life and turning to Jesus? Such hope is no hope at all. Let us place no confidence in the ability of the stony heart to want the Savior. But we have every reason to hope in a God who is mighty to save—before whom no heart is too hard and no life too far gone to escape His loving pursuit of grace.

# OBJECTION #9

## Election Is All about Israel

When Paul speaks of election in chapters 8 and 9 of the book of Romans, some have argued that he is talking about nations rather than individuals.[25] This objection was mentioned briefly back in chapter 4, but I would like to address it more fully here. Truly, God chose the Jewish nation as His own special people. "You [Israel] are a holy people to the LORD your God, and the LORD has chosen you to be a people for Himself, a special treasure above all the peoples who are on the face of the earth" (Deuteronomy 14:2). So, then, are all election passages referring to God's choice of national Israel? That is the objection sometimes raised. But regardless of whom Paul is speaking about in Romans 9, there are other election passages where gentiles are clearly being addressed.

| Scriptures Referring to the Election of the Gentiles |
| --- |
| But we are bound to give thanks to God always for you, brethren beloved by the Lord, because God *from the beginning chose you for salvation* through sanctification by the Spirit and belief in the truth. (2 Thessalonians 2:13) |
| In Him also we have obtained an inheritance, being predestined according to the purpose of Him who works all things according to the counsel of His will. (Ephesians 1:11) |
| Now when *the Gentiles* heard this, they were glad and glorified the word of the Lord. And as many as had been *appointed to eternal life* believed. (Acts 13:48) |

Each of the three passages above refers to God's choice of gentiles for salvation. The congregations in Thessalonica and Ephesus were primarily composed of non-Jews. Acts 13:48 explicitly states that certain gentiles were *appointed* (predestined) *to eternal life*. The argument that election is restricted to God's choice of Israel alone cannot be maintained in the face of these gentile election passages. Paul plainly told the gentile Thessalonians that they had been chosen by God for salvation.

But now, let us turn our attention to the election of Israel as a nation. Does this truth negate the election of individuals for salvation? Not at all because every nation is made up of individuals. The very origin of Israel's election began with the election of one man. "You are the LORD God, who *chose* Abram" (Nehemiah 9:7). God chose Abraham and said to him, "I will make you a great nation; I will bless you" (Genesis 12:2).

God's decision to bless a nation began with His choice to bless a single individual. And how could it be any other way? The whole does not exist in isolation from its parts. How can God choose to save a nation without, at some point, also choosing to save individual citizens of that nation? If God chose Israel, then the individual Israelite can truly say, "I am chosen." We see that principle in Romans where Paul speaks of individuals by name. "Just as it is written: "Jacob I have loved, but Esau I have hated" (Romans 9:13). Yes, indeed, the twin boys, Jacob and Esau, represented two nations in the womb of Rebekah (Genesis 25:23). But God still chose a man named Jacob. The chosen nation was made up of chosen people. God loved Jacob—Jacob, the individual man.

And why was the nation of Israel chosen by God? Was it owing to any quality found in them? Was it because Israel was greater than other nations? God tells us otherwise. "The Lord did not set His love on you nor choose you because you were more in number than any other people, for you were the least of all peoples; *but because the Lord loves you*, and because He would keep the oath which He swore to your fathers, the Lord has brought you out with a mighty hand, and redeemed you from the house of bondage" (Deuteronomy 7:7–8). God clarifies that His election of Israel had nothing to do with Israel. They were not better than any of the other nations. He loved them just because He loved them. God's choice of Israel was unconditional. That's the way election always works! Whether it be God's choice of a nation, the individual Jacob within that nation, or the Thessalonian gentile Christian—God loves them just because He loves them.

That was Paul's whole point in Romans 9. He is using the example of how election works in one case to show us how it works in every case—including individual election. The fact that Paul names another individual who is not elect (Pharaoh, Romans 9:17) demonstrates that he is discussing how personal election works. Paul also anticipates the objection someone might raise to individual election: "One of You will say, . . . 'Why have You made me like this?'" (Romans 9:19–20). It doesn't fit. Paul teaches us that God chose a nation, and someone objects, "Why did God make *me* like this?" Why would anyone raise that complaint to the election of a nation? The objection only makes sense if Paul is discussing the election of individuals.

## Who Art Thou, O Man?

Dealing with a difficult subject like election requires careful thought, study, and prayer. Asking questions and raising honest objections can be helpful in the process of understanding. It is good to come to the doctrine of election with a *Berean spirit*, searching the Scriptures to see if these things are true (Acts 17:11).

But I want to end this chapter with a note of caution. Let us not forget that above all our searching, questioning, and skepticism is a Sovereign. We must take care not to subtly elevate our questions and objections to a position of judgment over God's ways. We will never fully understand all His workings. Yet still, the Potter has rights over the clay, to shape, use, and dispose of the clay as is fitting to the Potter. Our lack of understanding is not a license for the clay to cast a shadow over the Potter's purpose and methods. The rebuke of the apostle reminds us to pause and take care when we question our Maker, "But indeed, O man, who are you to reply against God?" (Romans 9:20). Suppose you found an objection to sovereign election not covered in this chapter, or anywhere else for that matter. It seems ironclad, and no one can answer it. It stumps every expert and confounds the greatest minds of men. In the final analysis, what will this have achieved—except to set yourself at war with an electing God?

# CHAPTER 6

# WHY DOES IT MATTER?

I was finishing up a teaching series on the subject of the divine initiative. One woman in the class was clearly struggling with the whole matter. She reached a point of frustration and exclaimed, "Why does any of this matter?" She went on to explain that subjects like election are for theologians in seminary to ponder. But for the rest of us ordinary Christians, it has no relevance. She is not alone in her thinking. Many have come to this subject not with objections but with shrugged shoulders. In this teaching, they see no practical benefit for the life of the church and the daily devotion of following Jesus. Others simply avoid the topic for fear of controversy.

So then, why does this matter? I am convinced that embracing God's sovereign choice in salvation is good for our souls and binds us deeper to the Savior. I believe that election is good for us because God put it in His Word. There are a lot of things that God could have talked about in His Word but didn't. What He *did* put there is for our benefit. To say that any portion of God's Word is not relevant to my life is to suggest that God is a dispenser of trivia. Every word of Scripture is graciously given by God because He knows we have need of it. As believers, it is our highest aim to know God as an end in itself. We need no other benefit from these truths than the sheer delight of knowing Him more fully. That being said, knowing that God has chosen us for salvation produces an enormous benefit to our daily Christian experience.

Election is a doctrine, and for some believers, "doctrine" is a bad word. The complaint arises, "Don't give me all that doctrine—just give me Jesus!" But doctrine is simply the truth about God. The goal of doctrine is not merely knowledge but a renewing of the mind—leading to an internal transformation that changes how we live (Romans 12:2). Knowing the truth about God is the engine that drives worship, passion, and obedience in our daily Christian experience. What could be more practical than that? So then, let me share with you some reasons why the doctrine of election matters for everyday Christian living.

## It Matters to Suffering

I'm guessing you didn't expect me to begin with suffering. But "we must through many tribulations enter the kingdom of God" (Acts 14:22). That is the reality of taking up our cross daily and following Him. There is perhaps no other time where we are more likely to look to heaven for practical help than when we suffer. It is those dark moments of sorrow that move us more than anything to search God's Word for answers that will carry us through the pain.

You may think the doctrine of the election is the last thing you need to ponder when you are crying, but the apostle Paul thought otherwise. What prompted Paul to introduce his greatest commentary on divine election at the end of Romans 8? What brought the thought of predestination to his mind, beginning in verse 28 and on into chapter 9? Was it a desire to write a scholarly thesis for theologians to debate and contemplate? No. This was not a PhD dissertation but a letter written to rank-and-file Christians like you and me. Paul thought these ordinary Christians needed to know about election, and the subject that moved him there was *suffering.* "I consider that the sufferings of this present time are not worthy to be compared with the glory which will be revealed in us" (Romans 8:18).[26] Don't miss this. The Holy Spirit inspired motive that launched the greatest exposition of election in all of Scripture was to encourage hurting Christians.

When you are crying, you need to know a sovereign plan is behind your pain. You need to be assured that your suffering is not a detour from that plan, but God is still bringing about His good end with unstoppable energy. Though your suffering seems to shout, "Forsaken!" you need to know you have been eternally loved, pursued, and chosen by God. You need to hear that His predestined agenda is working out even this present suffering for your eternal good (Romans 8:28). God revealed the inner workings of His choice in salvation not to make us scratch our heads but to encourage us in the darkest times. It is a deep comfort to know that if He loved me like this before I was even born, He sure isn't going to quit on me now.

## It Matters to Assurance

Christian, how do you know you will still be following Jesus tomorrow? How can you be sure you will endure in faith next year and every year after that until you are safe in the glory world? You may be strong in faith today, but what about ten years from now? We do not know what trials the future may hold. Around the next turn may lie the circumstance that has the power to shake convictions and unravel certainty. According to Scripture, we do not know ourselves as well as we may think. We have scarcely understood our full capacity for sin. In our delusion, we boast, "I'm just a mediocre sinner. The really big sins are beyond my capability. And I would certainly never walk away from Jesus." But given the right temptation, the right amount of stress, and the right opportunity, sin will take us further than we ever thought possible. Jesus taught that saving faith is only that which endures to the end (Matthew 24:13). How, then, can we be sure that our faith will last? It is because we are safe in the plan.

One of the great implications of the divine initiative is the divine finish. Because God makes the first move, you can be assured He will make the last move as well. God is both the author and *finisher* of our faith (Hebrews 12:2).

The divine initiative says that your salvation is part of an eternal plan that cannot fail to succeed. "In Him also we *have obtained an inheritance*, being predestined according to the purpose of Him who works all things according to the counsel of His will" (Ephesians 1:11). Every believer has been swept up in a plan to which God is bringing all His omnipotence to bear. He is twisting and turning and designing and restraining and changing and working everything that happens into conformity to His purposes.

Do you know what that means, believer? You are safe in the plan! If you are in Christ, then you are in the plan. And if you are in the plan, then you are safe in the plan. Christian, God did not choose you, only to later lose you. You can have confidence that "He who has begun a good work in you will complete it until the day of Jesus Christ" (Philippians 1:6). After going through all the effort to bring the elect to faith by omnipotent power, will God now leave the final outcome to human strength? Not a chance! God will ensure that all His sheep remain in faith until they are safely in the fold. He who brought the elect to Christ will also cause them to endure in Christ until the end.

Consider how you came to know Christ in the first place. You were dead. God did it all. He did it without your help. So then, just as your coming to Christ was not accomplished by your power, your remaining in Christ is the same. The same God who wrought faith in you will sustain and secure everything necessary to complete His plan. "Having believed, you were sealed with the Holy Spirit of promise" (Ephesians 1:13).

Believer, Omnipotence has set His hand on you! He is "able to keep you from stumbling, and to present you faultless before the presence of His glory with exceeding joy" (Jude v. 24).

Not only will God cause His people to continue in faith but in holiness as well. "Without holiness no one will see the Lord" (Hebrews 12:14 NIV). Saving faith is demonstrated by a life of godliness. God will cause His elect to endure in this holiness. The same God who promises to give us a new heart also promises to move us to holy obedience: "I will give you a new heart and put a new spirit within you; I will take the heart of stone out of your flesh and give you a heart of flesh. I will put My Spirit within you and *cause you to walk in My statutes*, and you will keep My judgments and do them" (Ezekiel 36:26–27).

This is not to say that the sheep will never wander—they do! But there is a Good Shepherd who leads them back and keeps them safe: "My sheep hear My voice, and I know them, and they follow Me. And I give them eternal life, and they shall never perish; neither shall anyone snatch them out of My hand" (John 10:27–28).

On an airplane somewhere over the Atlantic Ocean, I struck up a conversation with the passenger sitting next to me. She was an elderly Christian woman who believed it was possible to lose salvation. I shared with her some Scriptures to which she seemed surprised to hear. Then I asked her, "Suppose there were a salvation in Christ that is totally secure. If there were a salvation that could not fail to save you, would you want that?" She eagerly exclaimed, "Yes!" In a flash, her heart spurned a salvation that depended on her flesh to maintain. Instinctively, she yearned for a redemption that was firm and unshakable. Dear reader, there is such a salvation. There is such a gospel. There is such a God who saves you like that. Though you grieved His heart by a thousand falls, He set His electing love on you. He gave up His only Son to purchase you. He changed your heart and gave you the gift of faith. He will now keep His purchased possession safe until the end. Are you among that blessed number who believe on the Son? Then you can say right now, "I am safe in the plan!"

## It Matters to Kingdom Building

In addition to your own personal security, this place of absolute assurance in the plan of God creates a solid platform for godly risk-taking. When you know that you are safe in the plan, it sets you free to step out in faith for His kingdom's sake. Safe in His hand is the place from which you can open your hand. Taking a risk for the kingdom of God is possible when everything that matters can't be lost and everything else is a gain to lose.

It is this confidence in the divine initiative that moved a small ship across the Aegean Sea in what was arguably the most significant voyage in human history. On his arrival in Neapolis, the apostle Paul brought the gospel to the European continent for the first time. The missionary journeys of Paul were laden with risk. What moved him to step into danger rather than comfort? It was the certainty of God's electing plan. "A vision appeared to Paul in the night. A man of Macedonia stood and pleaded with him, saying, 'Come over to Macedonia and help us'" (Acts 16:9). Paul crossed the Aegean and traveled thousands of miles under this conviction: not only had he been chosen by Christ to preach the gospel but God had an elect people waiting to hear the gospel. "I endure all things *for the sake of the elect*" (2 Timothy 2:10) was Paul's own justification for the hazards he undertook for the kingdom.

Jesus said, "And other sheep I have which are not of this fold; them also I must bring, and they will hear My voice; and there will be one flock and one shepherd" (John 10:16). When the Lord said this, the gospel had not yet traveled beyond Palestine, yet He spoke with certainty of sheep that were outside of the Jewish fold. He did not speak of maybes and possibilities but said, "Other sheep I have. . . I must bring them . . . they will hear. . . there will be one flock." This certainty of Christ's successful gathering has set free the feet of countless Christians to take the message of Jesus Christ to the lost. Hands and feet are liberated by the truth that His plan to gather the sheep cannot fail. Kingdom risk is possible when you are assured that not only are *you* safe in the plan but other sheep are within its grasp too, waiting for you to bring them the good news.[27]

## It Matters to Worship

In 1924 at Mount Wilson Observatory, Edwin Hubble peered through his telescope and made an astonishing discovery. What was previously thought to be clouds of gas and dust were, in fact, galaxies external to our own. Up until that time, scientists believed that the Milky Way represented the entire universe. Hubble's discovery revealed that our galaxy is just one among billions. The universe had not changed except in our minds. In a moment, the boundaries of the universe became much, much bigger. So too, when the sight of a sovereign, electing God enters our view, God becomes infinitely bigger in our eyes.

Our view of God does not change Him in any way, but it changes us profoundly. God is big. It is vital to our worship that we keep God big in our eyes. The greater our view of God, the higher our delight and satisfaction in Him will be. Worship is a response to what we see in God. It is to see God for who He is and then give back to Him that which is His due. Therefore, worship is directly connected to the boundaries of our God-view. One of the things the truth of election will bring to the believer is a great expansion of that view.

This is not to suggest that Christians do not worship God if they do not understand or agree with this truth. I am privileged to know many Christians who do not embrace the divine initiative in salvation. Their love and great affection for the Lord is clearly seen in their worship. But surely we can all agree that the more we know of God, the higher our worship will climb.

When the psalmist looked up at the stars and contemplated that God calls them all by name (Psalm 147:4), it moved him to worship. In his pre-Hubble view, the night sky was a much smaller place. He stood in awe that God could name thousands of stars. No doubt his worship would have been even higher had he contemplated the Governor of trillions upon trillions of worlds.

Every revelation that God discloses about Himself has worship as its goal. This truth that God made the first move to choose a people for salvation was revealed by God to create doxology. This truth was meant to produce hallelujahs! What moved Paul to burst into praise as he penned the first chapter of Ephesians? It was the truth of election that lifted His worship high.

> Blessed be the God and Father of our Lord Jesus Christ, who has blessed us with every spiritual blessing in the heavenly places in Christ, just as He chose us in Him before the foundation of the world, that we should be holy and without blame before Him in love. (Ephesians 1:3–4)

Try to say that sentence in a dull, monotone voice, and it just doesn't fit. These words are bursting with delight in God. Do not miss this. When Paul and the other biblical writers talk about God choosing us for salvation, it moved them to worship and praise. Does it do the same when you talk about it? When you think about God choosing you, are you moved to doxology as Paul was? Does your understanding of election ("He's just talking about Israel" or "God chose me because He looked ahead in time and saw me choosing Him") produce worship in your heart? Paul's understanding of election moved him to worship God. Should it not do the same for us? Oh, brothers and sisters, let God be God. Though election is laden with paradoxes and implications, let the Scripture just say what it looks like it is saying and bow down before Him in awe. Please do not get so bogged down in the mystery of it all that you miss the opportunity to praise Him. This truth is meant to produce hallelujahs!

The day I lifted my hand at a youth retreat marked the beginning of a life of worship. And like every believer, it was a worship that was meant to grow bigger as God expanded in my view. Knowing that

God makes the first move in salvation is just one of many revelations that have the power to move our worship deeper and higher. The truth of sovereign election is not the end itself but one of many windows through which we may gaze upon the beauty of God. Though the view through this window is magnificent, it is only a glimpse of His glory. How high our worship will soar when we catch that first full view of the King of Kings! Revelation 17:14 describes who will be there to see it: “those who are with Him are called, *chosen*, and faithful”—with every hand raised.

# Appendix A

# Difficult Passages

# John 3:16

**For God so loved the world that He gave His only begotten Son, that whoever believes in Him should not perish but have everlasting life.**

There is no passage of Scripture to which the divine initiative needs to be ashamed, but some passages seem (at first) to be inconsistent with this teaching. When believers are first exposed to divine election, the number one passage that comes to mind is John 3:16. For them, this passage is the death knell to God's sovereign choice in salvation because it clearly says that God loves the *whole world*. Let's look at it closely.

Firstly, how much does this passage tell us about election? Nothing. Not one thing. Election is not mentioned in this passage. In Scripture, God does not say everything in every verse. Rather, the whole revelation of God on a particular subject is scattered in many passages from Genesis to Revelation. Some passages speak to one issue while others address a different matter. John 3:16 is a wonderful word from God that is soaked in truth. But *all* the truth of God is not contained in this single verse. We are not taught anything about sanctification in this passage. God does not tell us in John 3:16 about the second coming of Christ or what heaven will be like. What is also absent from this passage is any teaching about election.

To be sure, this passage identifies the group of people who will have eternal life—whoever *believes* in the Son. But this verse says nothing about *who* will believe. A clear description is being given of those who will not perish. They are those who have faith in Christ. But who will come to faith in Christ and how will they come to that faith is simply not discussed in this passage. All the elect will, at some point in their life, believe in the Son. Jesus says, "All that the Father gives Me *will come* to Me." (John 6:37). Who is among this blessed company of people who will believe and not perish? God's Word tells us who they are: "And as many as had been appointed to eternal life believed" (Acts 13:48). So, to the truth of John 3:16, every person who embraces God's sovereign election says, "Amen!" Whoever believes in the Son will not perish. Whoever believes in the Son will have eternal life. And all the elect will do just that. All the rest will not.

But now, let's focus on the word "world" in John 3:16. That word creates a picture in our modern mind quite different from the image the ancients considered. When we think of the world, we cannot help but see all of it. We have seen pictures of the earth from space. We live every day in a global economy where everyone is connected by the internet. We can pull out our smartphone and talk to someone on the other side of the planet and think nothing of it. It comes as no surprise, therefore, when the modern reader assumes that John's world includes every human being that has ever lived. But the New Testament writers speak of the world in many different ways.

For example, we are told that "it came to pass in those days that a decree went out from Caesar Augustus that all the world should be registered" (Luke 2:1). Who was included in this world that Caesar registered? The ancient Chinese were not included, nor were the Mayans living in Central America. It is the *Roman world* that Luke had in mind. "World" does not always have to mean, and often does not mean, the totality of the human population. The Pharisees lamented in John 12:19, "Look, the whole world has gone after Him!" But they did not mean everybody. They themselves had not followed Jesus. It was a figure of speech. John himself refers to the world in at least ten different ways. Jesus said to His disciples, "If the world hates you, you know that it hated Me before it hated you" (John 15:18). Clearly, Jesus did not mean everybody on earth (including believers) hate Jesus and His followers. The world, in this context, was the *unbelieving world*.

So then the question we bring to John 3:16 is this: What did John mean by "world" in this passage? To understand the answer, we must consider what an amazing thing it was to the early church that gentiles were included in God's salvation. John was a Jew, as were most of the early followers of Jesus. By far, the biggest theological issue of the early church was the inclusion of the gentiles in the blessings won by the Messiah. The idea that salvation reaches beyond Israel to people from every nation was an astonishing reality to the early Jewish Christians. For Nicodemus and his contemporaries, God's love was directed exclusively to the people of Israel. The shocking declaration of John 3:16 is that God's love extends to the *gentile world*. The "whoevers" will come out of every tribe, tongue, and nation. The incredible gift of the Son is available to Jew and gentile alike. This revolutionary statement is made in the light of Jesus' previous declaration that "the wind blows where it wishes" (John 3:8). It is God's sovereign prerogative to extend His love beyond the borders of Palestine. The objects of His saving love will originate from every nation.

Finally, let's think about that word "whoever," or as it is translated in the King James Version, "whosoever." It is common to force upon this word the idea of potential. "Whoever believes in Him" is often understood to mean that there is the potential for any person (elect or not) to want Jesus. You may be surprised to hear that the word "whoever" is not in the original Greek of John 3:16.[28] In the original language, it says literally, "everyone believing," or "every believing one." This is not some potential in the non-elect to want what they do not want. This is the description of every soul who has been born from above. This is what born-again people do. They believe. God has indeed loved this world. He has presented His Son to every nation as the merciful rescue for those who would not perish. Whoever believes—whoever wants the Son, desires the Son, runs to the Son, trusts in the Son—will have everlasting life. That is a perfect description of the elect.

# 2 Peter 3:9

**The Lord is not slack concerning His promise, as some count slackness, but is longsuffering toward us, not willing that any should perish but that all should come to repentance.**

This passage is Peter's response to an objection about the second coming of Christ. The objection comes from "scoffers" who will rise up in the last days and say, "Where is the promise of His coming?" (2 Peter 3:3). The apostle points to the patience of God as the answer to this criticism. It is the patient mercy of God that explains the long delay in His coming. Peter clarifies the reason for this patience: God is "not willing that any should perish but that all should come to repentance." This passage teaches that the Lord restrains His coming in judgment to allow more time for repentance and salvation. At first glance, it seems Peter is suggesting that God does not choose a particular group of people for salvation. He desires all people to be saved.

The will of God is clearly in view here when Peter uses the word "willing." What God *wants* or *wills* about salvation is before us. Put negatively, God does not will that *any* perish. Put positively, it is the will of God that *all* would repent. This passage, therefore, hinges on two words—"any" and "all."

Who is included in the words "any" and "all"? The answer to that question will reveal what God wills about salvation in this portion of Scripture. But wait! The answer is obvious, isn't it? "Any" and "all" includes everyone. But how do we use these words in everyday conversation? Suppose the boss asks at the start of a meeting, "Are we all here?" Is he asking if the entirety of the human race is present? No one would interpret his question in that way. His use of "all" is limited to all the people within a particular group—in this case, the group of employees who were invited to the meeting. If a friend asks you, "Do you think anybody will come to the class reunion this year?" You would automatically understand "anybody" to be limited to former classmates. You would not expect anybody to include people who are not alumni.

When we hear the words "any" and "all," we instinctively search the context to determine the group of people being referenced. Any-who? All of whom? It could be every human being. It could indicate any person on earth. It could also be limited to a smaller group. Who gets to answer these questions? Peter does.

To what group of people is this letter addressed? In the first letter of Peter, he describes the group of people he is writing to as "*elect* according to the foreknowledge of God the Father" (1 Peter 1:2). Peter confirms that he is writing to the same group of people in the second letter: "Beloved, I now write to you this second epistle" (2 Peter 3:1). So in 2 Peter 3:9, to what group of people is God being "patient and longsuffering with"? It is the elect. The reason God is patient with His return is that He is not willing that any *of His elect* would perish. God wants all *of His elect* to come to repentance. Jesus Christ has a chosen flock of sheep scattered across history. Some of them have not yet been born. He will not return in judgment until every last one of them has come to Him in repentance. Seen in its proper context, this statement of Peter is not in conflict with the divine initiative. Quite the contrary, it is one of the most powerful statements in Scripture to support it.

But some may still insist that "all" includes all human beings who have ever lived. Let's think through the implications of that, and it will be quickly apparent how unworkable that notion is. If it is the sovereign will of God that *all* human beings are saved, then hell would be empty and no one would be lost. If that is the case, then this verse would prove universalism, not the gospel. Christians who press this interpretation of 2 Peter 3:9 are proving more than they wanted. The objection rises, "Yes, God wills every human being who has ever lived to be saved, but some thwarted His will with unbelief and are lost." This view of the text renders God helpless and unable to accomplish what He wants. God wanted all humans to be saved but did not get what He wanted—a far cry from the God of Psalm 115:3 who "does whatever He pleases." If you press this text to include all human beings who have ever lived, you end up with either universalism or an impotent God. But the God of 2 Peter 3:9 is patiently working out a plan to accomplish all His will. He patiently delays His coming so that not one of His elect will be lost.

# 1 Timothy 2:3–4

**For this is good and acceptable in the sight of God our Savior, who desires all men to be saved and to come to the knowledge of the truth.**

The gospel of Jesus Christ transcends all boundaries of race, class, and social status. Calvary is the great leveler. Kings and beggars stand equal in the shadow of the cross. From the church in Ephesus (to which Timothy belonged) to the modern church, the temptation of every congregation is to restrict the gospel to people who look just like us. It seems to be our default mode to gravitate toward people who share the same class, race, and background as ourselves.

This word to Timothy is a reminder that the gospel is for people of every position in society. Paul precedes this verse with a plea for prayer: "Therefore I exhort first of all that supplications, prayers, intercessions, and giving of thanks be made for all men" (1 Timothy 2:1). The apostle then clarifies who "all men" is: "for kings and all who are in authority, that we may lead a quiet and peaceable life in all godliness and reverence (1 Timothy 2:2). Timothy is being instructed to pray for people in positions of authority and power. Prayer is not to be limited to any one class of people but is to be offered up to God on behalf of everyone—even kings. It is in this context we are told that "this [praying for kings] is good and acceptable in the sight of God our Savior, who desires all men to be saved" (1 Timothy 2:3–4). The "all men" in this text is *all kinds* of men. Paul is telling Timothy to pray for people of every social status—even kings and rulers.[29] What is being discussed here is not the salvation of every person on earth but every class of humanity. The gospel is for people in every station. The elect will be gathered from both the poor and the rich, male and female, Jew and gentile, kings and peasants. It pleases God our Savior to make up His church from every walk of life. The church at Ephesus and the church on Main Street must, therefore, make every effort to pray, evangelize, and love across social, racial, and economic boundaries.

# Ezekiel 33:11

**"As I live," says the Lord God, "I have no pleasure in the death of the wicked, but that the wicked turn from his way and live."**

What people want at any point in time is . . . complicated. I want to eat french fries on a regular basis. I also want to keep my cholesterol low. I want to sleep in. But I don't want to be late for work. When faced with what I want, I often find there is competition for that spot. Competing desires fight within me for first place. The desire that rises highest will be the one that determines my actions. My will at any moment is the desire that ascends higher than all others. I am not alone in this complexity of the will. In each of us, there is a hierarchy of desire. Our choice will always be our highest will for the moment.

Take a judge, for example, who must pronounce sentence over a young man who stole a car. His will on the matter is complicated. There is a desire to give justice to the owner of the car. Also present is the desire to protect the public from crime. Alongside these is the desire to show mercy to a messed-up kid who made a stupid choice. Which desire is what the judge *wants*? All of them. We can truly say the judge wants the young man to go free with a stern warning. We can also say the judge wants the man to be punished with a stiff sentence. Upon which desire will he act? His decision will be determined by the desire that rises to first place. When the judge sentences the man to prison, it is because his desire for justice rose higher than his compassion for the young man. The actions of every thinking being are determined by the desire that ascends highest and promises the greatest overall benefit. Lesser wants are routinely set aside for higher wants.

God says through the prophet Ezekiel, "I have no pleasure in the death of the wicked, but that the wicked turn from his way and live." In this passage, God plainly states that it is not His will for the wicked to die. And yet we discover in 1 Samuel 2:25 concerning the wicked sons of Eli that "the Lord desired to kill them." We are also told in Romans 9:18 that God "has mercy on whom He wills, and whom He wills He hardens." So, what does God want? Does He want the wicked sons of Eli to turn from their sin and live, or does He want them to die? Does He want all people to repent, or does He want some people to be hardened? The answer is yes. There is a sense in which God wants all people saved. There is also a sense in which God wants some people hardened. The desire that God acts on is the one that rises to the highest place.

The Bible often describes God as wanting something in one way that He does not want in another way. Each one of these perspectives is the true will of God and represents a window into His heart. At first glance, however, they appear contradictory.

| **God desires in one way what He does not desire in another way.** | |
|---|---|
| I have no pleasure in the death of the wicked.<br>Ezekiel 33:11 | The Lord desired to kill them.<br>1 Samuel 2:25 |
| Repent, for the kingdom of heaven is at hand!<br>Matthew 3:2 | Whom He wills He hardens.<br>Romans 9:18 |
| You hate all workers of iniquity.<br>Psalm 5:5 | For God so loved the world that He gave His only begotten Son.<br>John 3:16 |

Every believer of the Bible must wrestle with this apparent duplicity in the will of God. Is God schizophrenic? Hardly. What seems like a contradiction is but the complexity of desire that exists in any thinking being. The multiple perspectives of your own will is but a tiny pool compared to the deep ocean of God's perfect will. As is true of your desires (though infinitely holier and more complex), God wants things in one way that He does not want in another way. Upon which desire does He ultimately act? God will act on the desire that rises highest to give Him maximum glory. This is His *sovereign will*.

There is something that God wants that cannot be stopped (Isaiah 14:27), and it is always accomplished (Isaiah 46:10). Everything that happens is made to work in its favor (Ephesians 1:11). It is God's sovereign will for history. It is the desire of God that rises to the highest place in His heart so that He always acts on it and ensures its success. Other desires of God He will allow to be broken for the moment. But God always gets His sovereign will.

When Pilate delivered Jesus to the cross, He broke the will of God, who detests when the innocent are condemned (Proverbs 17:15). God desires that judges rule justly. In this case, God could have gotten what He wanted in a thousand ways. He could have made sure that Pilate was never governor in the first place. He could have caused a fair and impartial judge to ascend to the position of procurator. Yet God did not act on His desire for justice. He postponed His will in this matter, allowing Pilate to act corruptly for the moment, because He had a higher want—His sovereign will. "You anointed . . . Pilate . . . to do whatever Your hand and Your purpose determined before to be done" (Acts 4:28).

Ezekiel 33:11 says that God does not want wicked people to die. He longs for them to turn from their wicked way and live. This is God's will. But is it God's highest will that no wicked people die? Is this the want that rises to the highest place and is always accomplished? If it were God's sovereign will that all people would repent, then hell would be empty.

The Bible teaches that, in the end, some will not be saved. In fact, we are told that many will be lost (Matthew 7:13). Either God is incapable of getting what He wants, or something else is going on here. Like the earthly judge that had genuine compassion for the young man but sent him to prison anyway, God chooses not to act on some desires to achieve a greater desire.

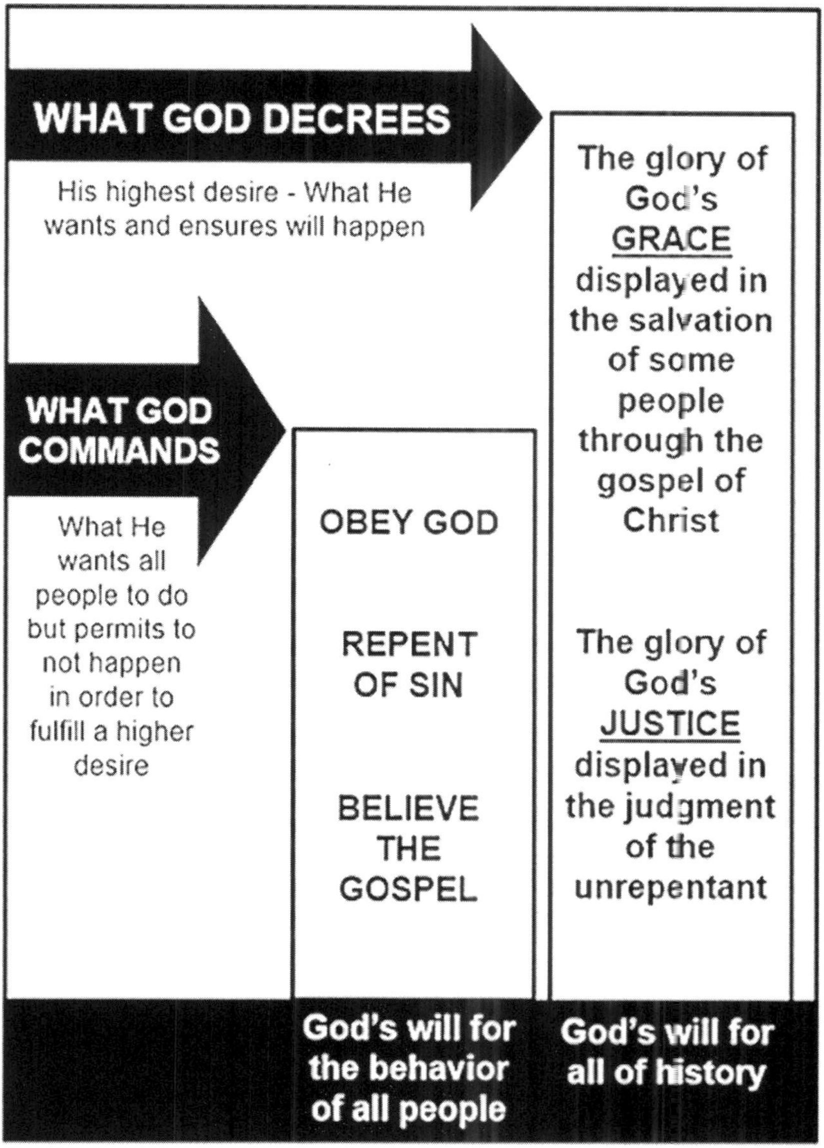
WHAT GOD DECREES
His highest desire - What He wants and ensures will happen
WHAT GOD COMMANDS
What He wants all people to do but permits to not happen in order to fulfill a higher desire
OBEY GOD
REPENT OF SIN
BELIEVE THE GOSPEL
The glory of God's GRACE displayed in the salvation of some people through the gospel of Christ
The glory of God's JUSTICE displayed in the judgment of the unrepentant
God's will for the behavior of all people
God's will for all of history

Ezekiel 33:11 is a beautiful window into the heart of God. God truly wants all people to repent. He does not take sadistic pleasure in the destruction of the wicked. We see this disposition in God as Jesus wept over Jerusalem (Matthew 23:37). He longed to gather them, but they were not willing. The heart of God truly desires that people everywhere would turn from their sin. But that universal desire for repentance in no way prevents God from pursuing a higher desire that will bring Him more glory. More glory than the repentance of all people? Yes. God gains maximum glory through the salvation of some people to the praise of His glorious grace and the judgment of other people to the praise of His glorious justice. God will subordinate all other desires to achieve this highest delight. This in no way negates His compassion for lost people—all of them. He genuinely desires that all people would turn from sin and not perish. At the same time, God has a higher will to put the glory of His grace on open display in the gospel. He ensures the success of His highest desire by electing some to salvation and granting them a new heart. These will then gladly turn from their ways, look to Christ, and live.

# 1 John 4:14

**And we have seen and testify that the Father has sent the Son as Savior of the world.**

How many saviors has God offered to the world? Only *one* name has been "given among men [mankind or the human race] by which we must be saved" (Acts 4:12). The Father has presented His Son as the solitary means by which people can be saved. Therefore, if anyone is saved, it will be through Christ alone.

If God provides a Savior for this world, does that prove He intends for everyone on earth to be saved? If we take this verse to mean that it is God's plan to save the whole world, then either universalism is true (God will ultimately save all people) or, if some are lost, God failed to accomplish His plan. If we say that God tried to save the whole world but could not because some people's free will would not yield, then the ultimate power in the universe is free will, and God is not God.

This verse in no way conflicts with the divine initiative of God to save an elect people. If God has chosen to save a people in this world, then of course He will provide a Savior for this world. This verse is not a record of the failure of God to accomplish His purposes. It is the triumph of God's initiative to save His church; He sent the Son—a provision has been made for the elect of all the earth to be redeemed.

Nor do we see in John's statement a declaration of universalism but actually an insistence on the exclusivity of the gospel. Christ is the only Savior that God has held out to this world. Anyone in the world, therefore, who would enter the kingdom must come through this door of Christ. By God's enabling grace, the elect from all the world will come to this blessed provision (John 6:37).

# John 12:32

**And I, if I am lifted up from the earth, will draw all peoples to Myself.**

Just two little words in this verse—"all peoples"—cause some folks to stumble over the divine initiative. The people who heard those words for the first time stumbled too—but not for the same reason. For them, this statement was a radical revelation concerning the scope of the Messiah's mission. The salvation of Christ is not for the people of Israel alone, but the elect of God would be drawn from every nation. *All peoples* (both Jew and gentile) are included in it.

Jesus was teaching in Jerusalem in the final days before the cross. It was the time of the Passover, and a group of men came up to the feast to worship, whom John describes as "Greeks" (John 12:20). The biblical writers sometimes referred to the gentiles as Greeks regardless of what nation they came from (Romans 3:9). It was a general nickname for anyone from outside the Jewish nation. These men were foreigners. They were proselytes to the God of Abraham who, like the Ethiopian of Acts 8:27, traveled a great distance to worship God at the temple. These converted gentiles would have been permitted to worship in the outer court of the temple known as the Court of the Gentiles. Though they had come from distant lands, even they had heard of Jesus and approached the disciples to gain an audience with Him.

The moment Andrew and Philip delivered their request, the heart of Jesus was troubled (John 12:27). News of Christ-seeking, gentile men instantly triggered a discussion of His death. "The hour has come that the Son of Man should be glorified" (John 12:23). Here standing before the Lord are men from outside Israel—gentile men who are *drawn* to the Savior. Their very presence was a graphic reminder of Jesus' mission on earth: to redeem a people from every nation. These are the sheep from *another fold* He came to gather into one flock (John 10:16). Jesus knew full well what that gathering would cost. He speaks of being "lifted up from the earth." John leaves no doubt as to what Jesus means by this lifting up. "This He said, signifying by what death He would die." (John 12:33). And what would be the result of this lifting up of Jesus on a cross? All peoples—all *kinds* of people—people from every tribe and nation—people like these Greeks—will be drawn to the Savior for salvation.[30]

Just as was found in the previous section concerning 1 Timothy 2:3–4, when we come across a universal term like "all," we must ask, "All what?" Everyone *within a particular category* is included in *all*. If that category is the entire human race, then we must conclude from this verse that every single person living after the cross is drawn to Jesus for salvation. That would include millions who lived in the Americas centuries before the gospel reached its shores. Were they drawn to the Son? It would also include the Pharisees who hated Jesus and plotted to kill Him (Matthew 12:14). Were they drawn as well? The problems pile up when we push the word "all" beyond what the context demands.

What was it that moved Father and Son to rejoice together in this passage? What caused the Son to lift up His eyes to heaven and bid His Father slay Him for His glory? It was the knowledge of a ransomed church made up of *all peoples*—each one effectually drawn from every nation to put the glory of God's grace on display.

# Romans 10:13

**For "whoever calls on the name of the LORD shall be saved."**

I include this passage as representative of many statements in the Bible where a general invitation is given to repent and turn to the Lord for salvation. There are a host of other similar passages such as Matthew 11:28, Joshua 24:15, and Revelation 22:17. Each of these passages pleads with the unbeliever to choose the salvation of God. To be sure, a genuine invitation is being given in Romans 10:13. Everyone who repents and believes in Jesus Christ will be saved. The door of salvation is open to all who will call. But *who* will call upon the Lord? Only the elect will do so. Only those hearts that have been regenerated by the Holy Spirit will answer this gracious summons to redemption. The invitation goes out to all, but only the elect will respond. As Jesus said, "Many are called, but few are chosen" (Matthew 22:14). The non-elect will harden their heart and reject the invitation.

Someone may ask, "What if a non-elect person calls on the Lord?" Such a person has demonstrated by their faith that they are among the elect! The non-elect will never choose to call on the Lord—because they do not want Him.

# Revelation 3:20

**Behold, I stand at the door and knock. If anyone hears My voice and opens the door, I will come in to him and dine with him, and he with Me.**

When I was a boy, hanging in our living room was a copy of "Christ at Heart's Door" by American artist Warner Sallman. In those days, this popular painting found its way into many people's homes, Sunday school classrooms, and family Bibles. It pictured a very Caucasian, gentle Jesus knocking on a door. I remember often staring into that scene and wondering about it. Jesus is not pushing His way inside. If you look closely at the painting, He doesn't even have a doorknob on His side—you must let Him in.

The painting is based on Revelation 3:20, where Jesus declares that He is knocking at the door, calling for those within to hear His voice and invite Him inside. I think perhaps the picture tells me little about what Jesus thinks and much about what *the artist* thinks. He, like many others, sees this passage as the call of God to the unbeliever. The Lord stands patiently knocking, but *you* must take the initiative to open the door. From this interpretation, man's free will is the decisive power in salvation.

If we pull this verse out of the surrounding context, it is easy to see why some might view it as a call to the unregenerate. But of course, we must not do that. We must come to this text (and every text of Scripture) in the light of everything around it. Who is being addressed in Revelation 3:20? On whose door is Jesus knocking? Who does Jesus gently plead with to invite Him inside? It is not the unbeliever—it is the church! John was told by the Lord to write these things "to the seven churches" (Revelation 1:11). In particular, this statement before us was addressed to the church in Laodicea.[31] Just two verses later, in Revelation 3:22, we are told, "He who has an ear, let him hear what the Spirit says *to the churches*." This is not a passage calling dead sinners to open up doors. This is a call to the living church—the elect whom God has made alive. Only the regenerate church of God has been enabled to open the door and fellowship with Christ. Going deeper into our relationship with Jesus does not happen before the new birth but after.

In this letter to the Laodicean church, Jesus warns them that they had become spiritually lukewarm. The passion they once knew was fading, but Jesus' love for them remained. It is this love that moves Jesus to rebuke them, discipline them, and call them to repentance: "As many as I love, I rebuke and chasten. Therefore be zealous and repent" (Revelation 3:19). He calls these Christians to open the door and return to the place of fellowship and nearness they once enjoyed with Christ.

Opening doors, repenting, hearing Jesus' voice, inviting Jesus into fellowship—these are the actions of the spiritually living. This is the business of sanctification that takes place every day among those who are born again. These are the words of the Savior to His church.

If Revelation 3:20 were addressed to the unregenerate, if Christ could do nothing but stand and wait for a corpse to open up the door, if salvation depended on the *human initiative*, Jesus would still be standing there waiting—for you and for me. But hallelujah for the *divine initiative*! Thanks be to God for sovereign love that chose us, sought us out, and made us alive in Christ. Now we hear Him knocking and gladly open the door.

# Appendix B

# Further Study

## We are born with a fallen nature.

"The wicked are estranged from the womb; They go astray as soon as they are born, speaking lies." (Psalm 58:3)

"Behold, I was brought forth in iniquity, And in sin my mother conceived me." (Psalm 51:5)

## The fallen person is spiritually dead.

"And you He made alive, who were dead in trespasses and sins." (Ephesians 2:1)

"And you, being dead in your trespasses and the uncircumcision of your flesh, He has made alive together with Him, having forgiven you all trespasses." (Colossians 2:13)

## The fallen person is unable to turn from sin and submit to God's law.

"Because the carnal mind is enmity against God; for it is not subject to the law of God, *nor indeed can be*." (Romans 8:7)

## The fallen person is unable to please God.

"So then, those who are in the flesh cannot please God." (Romans 8:8)

"For I know that in me (that is, in my flesh) nothing good dwells; for to will is present with me, but how to perform what is good I do not find." (Romans 7:18)

## The fallen person is a slave to sin and powerless to overcome it.

"Jesus answered them, 'Most assuredly, I say to you, whoever commits sin is a slave of sin.'" (John 8:34)

"For when we were still *without strength*, in due time Christ died for the ungodly." (Romans 5:6)

## The fallen person cannot understand the gospel.

"But the natural man does not receive the things of the Spirit of God, for they are foolishness to him; *nor can he know them*, because they are spiritually discerned." (1 Corinthians 2:14)

## Left unaided, the fallen person has no ability to repent and believe on Christ.

"No one can come to Me unless the Father who sent Me draws him." (John 6:44)

"It is the Spirit who gives life; the flesh profits nothing." (John 6:63)

"Therefore I have said to you that no one can come to Me unless it has been granted to him by my Father." (John 6:65)

"No one can say that Jesus is Lord except by the Holy Spirit." (1 Corinthians 12:3)

## Faith and repentance are gifts from God.

"Looking unto Jesus, the *author* and finisher of our faith" (Hebrews 12:2)

"Correcting those who are in opposition, If God perhaps will *grant them repentance*" (2 Timothy 2:25)

"For to you it has been *granted* on behalf of Christ, not only to *believe* in Him, but also to suffer for His sake." (Philippians 1:29)

## References of Jesus to a group of people the Father has "given to Him."

"This is the will of the Father who sent Me, that of all *He has given Me* I should lose nothing, but should raise it up at the last day." (John 6:39)

"My Father, who has *given them to Me*, is greater than all; and no one is able to snatch them out of My Father's hand." (John 10:29)

"You have given Him authority over all flesh, that He should give eternal life *to as many as You have given Him*." (John 17:2)

"I pray for them. I do not pray for the world but for those whom *You have given Me*." (John 17:9)

"Father, I desire that they also *whom You gave Me* may be with Me where I am, that they may behold My glory which You have given Me." (John 17:24)

## Other Scriptures referring to the elect:

| | | |
|---|---|---|
| Matthew 24:22 | Romans 8:33 | 1 Thess 1:4 |
| Matthew 24:24 | Romans 11:5 | Titus 1:1 |
| Matthew 24:31 | Romans 11:7 | 1 Peter 1:1 |
| Mark 13:20 | Romans 11:28 | 1 Peter 2:9 |
| Mark 13:22 | 2 Timothy 2:10 | 1 Peter 5:13 |

## God has chosen in advance a people for salvation.

"He chose us in Him before the foundation of the world, that we should be holy and without blame before Him in love, having predestined us to adoption as sons by Jesus Christ to Himself, according to the good pleasure of His will." (Ephesians 1:4–5)

"In Him also we have obtained an inheritance, being predestined according to the purpose of Him who works all things according to the counsel of His will." (Ephesians 1:11)

"For whom He foreknew, He also predestined to be conformed to the image of His Son, that He might be the firstborn among many brethren. Moreover whom He predestined, these He also called; whom He called, these He also justified; and whom He justified, these He also glorified." (Romans 8:29–30)

"When the Gentiles heard this, they were glad and glorified the word of the Lord. And *as many as had been appointed to eternal life* believed." (Acts 13:48)

"What if God, wanting to show His wrath and to make His power known, endured with much longsuffering the vessels of wrath prepared for destruction, and that He might make known the riches of His glory on the *vessels of mercy, which He had prepared beforehand for glory*." (Romans 9:22–24)

“Knowing, beloved brethren, your *election* by God.” (1 Thessalonians 1:4)

“God *from the beginning chose you for salvation* through sanctification by the Spirit and belief in the truth.” (2 Thessalonians 2:13)

“I know whom I have chosen.” (John 13:18)

## The new birth precedes and causes faith.

“Now a certain woman named Lydia heard us. She was a seller of purple from the city of Thyatira, who worshiped God. *The Lord opened her heart* to heed the things spoken by Paul.” (Acts 16:14)

“But God, who is rich in mercy, because of His great love with which He loved us, *even when we were dead* in trespasses, *made us alive* together with Christ (by grace you have been saved).” (Ephesians 2:4–5)

“Whoever believes that Jesus is the Christ *is* born of God.” (1 John 5:1)

**God's choice of the elect is not based on anything they have done or any quality foreseen in them.**

"For this is the word of promise: 'At this time I will come and Sarah shall have a son.' And not only this, but when Rebecca also had conceived by one man, even by our father Isaac (*for the children not yet being born, nor having done any good or evil, that the purpose of God according to election might stand, not of works but of Him who calls*), it was said to her, 'The older shall serve the younger.' As it is written, 'Jacob I have loved, but Esau I have hated.'" (Romans 9:9–13)

"Who has saved us and called us with a holy calling, *not according to our works*, but according to His own purpose and grace which was given to us in Christ Jesus *before time began.*" (2 Timothy 1:9)

"You did not choose Me, but I chose you." (John 15:16)

"So then *it is not of him who wills, nor of him who runs*, but of God who shows mercy." (Romans 9:16)

"For you see your calling . . . God has chosen the foolish things of the world to put to shame the wise, and God has chosen the weak things of the world . . . that no flesh should glory in His presence." (1 Corinthians 1:26–29)

# NOTES

## Chapter 1

[1] Gregory S. Neal, *Grace Upon Grace* (Bloomington, IN: Westbow, 2014), 15.

[2] Max Lucado, *Grace* (Nashville: Thomas Nelson, 2012), 118. The author argues that the reason behind God's election is that "there is something in you that God loves."

[3] A typical example of conditional election on the basis of God's foreknowledge is expressed in Norman Geisler, *Chosen But Free* (Minneapolis: Bethany House, 2010), 18.

[4] Charles H. Spurgeon, *Autobiography*, *Volume 1: The Early Years, 1834-1859* (Edinburgh: Banner of Truth, 1973), 165.

[5] A similar illustration is used in Charles H. Spurgeon, "Eternal Life," Chapel Library, 2001, London, www.spurgeongems.org.

## Chapter 2

[6] Elisabeth Elliot, *Passion and Purity* (Grand Rapids: Baker, 2002), 73. Paraphrased from a quote by Addison Leitch.

[7] The reasoning in this paragraph owes a great deal to and borrows heavily from R. C. Sproul, *Chosen by God* (Wheaton, IL: Tyndale, 1988), 92–94. I am forever grateful to the late Dr. Sproul for opening my eyes to the gospel of sovereign grace.

[8] Michael Horton, *Putting Amazing Back into Grace* (Grand Rapids: Baker, 2002), 46.

[9] D. A. Carson, *The Gospel According to John* (Grand Rapids: Eerdmans, 1991), 350.

[10] Illustration paraphrased from James Montgomery Boice, *Foundations of the Christians Faith: A Comprehensible & Readable Theology* (Downers Grove, IL: Intervarsity, 1986), 213.

## Chapter 3

[11] J. I. Packer, *Concise Theology* (Wheaton, IL: Tyndale, 1993), 170.

[12] Gary Willis, "'Born again' politics." *The New York Times,* August 1, 1976, https://nyti.ms/1LLtESu.

[13] Charles Leiter, *Justification and Regeneration* (Hannibal, MO: Granted Ministries, 2009), 66.

[14] Wayne Grudem, *Systematic Theology* (Grand Rapids: Zondervan, 1994), 699.

[15] Billy Graham, *How to Be Born Again* (Nashville: Thomas Nelson, 1977), 178.

[16] Sam Storms, *Chosen for Life* (Wheaton, IL: Crossway, 2007), 152.

[17] Anthony Hoekema, *Saved by Grace* (Grand Rapids: Eerdmans, 1994), 111.

[18] J. C. Ryle, *St. Luke, Vol. 2,* Expository Thoughts on the Gospels (New York: Carter & Brothers, 1875), 471.

## Chapter 4

[19] John Steinbeck, *Of Mice and Men* (New York: Penguin, 1993), 56–57.

[20] Steinbeck, 60.

[21] Steven Lawson, *The Kind of Preaching God Blesses* (Eugene, OR: Harvest House, 2013), 103.

[22] John Piper, *The Pleasures of God* (Sisters, OR: Multnomah, 2000), 130.

## Chapter 5

[23] Sproul, *Chosen by God*, 37. A similar illustration is used.

[24] J. I. Packer, *Knowing God* (Downers Grove, IL: InterVarsity, 1973), 79.

[25] Geisler, *Chosen But Free*, 165.

## Chapter 6

[26] Thomas Schreiner, *Romans* (Grand Rapids: Baker Academic, 1998), 454–455. A connection is made between present suffering in Romans 8:18 and the predestined glorification of the elect in Romans 8:28–29.

[27] John Piper, *Don't Waste Your Life* (Wheaton, IL: Crossway, 2003), 79–98. The concept of risk taking for the kingdom of God is discussed.

[28] R. K. McGregor Wright, *No Place for Sovereignty* (Downers Grove, IL: InterVarsity, 1996), 159.

[29] Keith Mathison, *Dispensationalism: Rightly Dividing the People of God?* (Phillipsburg, NJ: P&R, 1995), 66. The text is interpreted by the author as an admonition to pray for all kinds of men.

[30] D. A. Carson, *The Gospel According to John* (Grand Rapids: Eerdmans, 1991), 436–444. The author comes to the same conclusion. The gentile request to see Jesus was a trigger for 12:32, and "all peoples" is referring to the inclusion of the gentiles.

[31] John MacArthur, Revelation 1–11, *MacArthur New Testament Commentary* (Chicago: Moody, 1999), 140. The author points out that the door statement is addressed to the church at Laodicea and, consequently, to the church in general.

For a FREE copy of this book to share, visit

**ccc-press.com**

**David Ervin** is a follower of Jesus, husband to Katie, and pastor of Cornerstone Christian Church in Belleville, MI. He holds a BA from Columbia Evangelical Seminary, Longview, WA.

CCC Press

Belleville, Michigan